SLAVE LABOR
── *on* ──
VIRGINIA'S
BLUE RIDGE RAILROAD

SLAVE LABOR
— *on* —
VIRGINIA'S
BLUE RIDGE RAILROAD

MARY E. LYONS

THE
History
PRESS

Published by The History Press
Charleston, SC
www.historypress.com

First published 2020

Manufactured in the United States

ISBN 9781467144902

Library of Congress Control Number: 2019954252

To the memory of
Commander Joseph Eugene Lyons (1944–2019), U.S. Navy, retired,
who loved planes, ships and trains.

CONTENTS

PREFACE

Blue Ridge Railroad Papers at the Library of Virginia are organized in archival boxes containing folders stuffed with documents. None of the folders is conveniently labeled "slavery." My decade-long mission has been to uncover details about Blue Ridge Railroad enslavement that have been scattered through the files for more than 160 years. As I read and transcribed many hundreds of handwritten sheets of paper, I noted every fact about slave labor that surfaced. What I learned as of 2014 was published in *The Blue Ridge Tunnel: A Remarkable Engineering Feat in Antebellum Virginia.* More material appears in *The Virginia Blue Ridge Railroad*, published in 2015. *Slave Labor on Virginia's Blue Ridge Railroad* greatly expands the slavery content of the first two books and explores newly discovered documents.

Few specifics about the enslaved people's daily lives are known. Still, we can now gauge the nature of their grueling toil, where they labored along the line and who controlled them. Circumstances affecting Irish workers often impacted enslaved laborers. So that readers can understand this cause and effect, I trace the dizzying loop the loop of ever-changing contractors (see appendix 3), wage fluctuations and other events such as strikes and the cholera epidemic in 1854. To place slave labor in context, I have provided details about various aspects of the railroad construction. For the most part, this book is presented in chronological order, which I deem the most logical way of comprehending a public works project that proceeded along seventeen miles for ten years.

My ongoing task has been the naming of enslaved people (see appendix 4). Thankfully, a surviving set of state payrolls lists names of those who labored in the Blue Ridge Tunnel. Blue Ridge Railroad contracts show names of men and boys and the slaveholders who rented their labor for other parts of the line. Ledger books reveal the names of deliverymen. I harvested more names from receipts and other miscellaneous documents. The name of Hannah Harden, a woman enslaved by a Blue Ridge Railroad vendor, shows up in a collection of his papers at the Library of Virginia. These papers prove that her labor indirectly supported construction of the line.

Recently found newspaper articles feature the memories of James Williams, who was hired out to labor on the construction when he was twelve years old. The articles contain rare details and photographs. Presented herein, they are the only known first-person account and image of any laborer, enslaved or free, who toiled directly on the Blue Ridge Railroad.

For the remaining slaves, I have no names at all. Most of the contractors kept their own payrolls and probably discarded them after their jobs ended. The 1850 and 1860 federal slave schedules listed slaveholders' names and the age, gender and color of slaves—but no slave names. If a slaveholder hired out an enslaved person, the census enumerator sometimes included the name of the lessee on the same line that listed the owner. The information can be helpful for linking a slaveholder and unnamed enslaved person with a contractor's name—but only for the census years of 1850 and 1860. Slave schedules for the in-between years—most of the Blue Ridge Railroad construction period—do not exist.

After the great wall of slavery fell in 1865, full names of African Americans became part of the country's official records. In Reconstruction-era Freedmen's Bureau records, tax lists, federal censuses, marriage records and newspapers, first and last names appeared where they should have been all along. Many of the documents are available online, making it possible to trace the lives of some—but by no means all—formerly enslaved people, their families and their communities after emancipation.

ACKNOWLEDGEMENTS

For a residential and affiliate fellowship that has allowed research on the Blue Ridge Railroad for ten years, I give ongoing thanks to Virginia Humanities, located in Charlottesville, Virginia. A 2016 grant from the Railroad and Locomotive Historical Society—the oldest such organization in the country—permitted me to transcribe 130 primary documents from the Blue Ridge Railroad Papers at the Library of Virginia. The transcripts were invaluable for linking pieces of information about enslaved laborers that initially seemed unrelated.

I thank William T. Ellison Jr., a member of the audience during my presentation at the Waynesboro Public Library on October 9, 2018. He alerted me to a newspaper article about James Williams. Dale Brumfield, writer, generously forwarded all of his saved clippings on Williams before the day was over.

Sharing my excitement, dedicated researcher Jane C. Smith located more clippings and connected me with a living descendant of Thomas Jarman, original enslaver of James Williams. The descendant patiently shared with me everything he knew about his ancestors and Williams. Tom Carlsson of the Waynesboro Historical Commission kindly located a deed providing details about the farm that James Williams bought in 1893 and assisted with the photograph of Hannah Harden's gravestone.

Karen Vest, archivist at the Waynesboro Public Library, helped identify a photograph of Hannah Harden and gain permission to print it. Karen and the library's archives are rare treasures. I also thank Debra Weiss, who alerted

A Blue Ridge Tunnel Foundation board member explores the Dove Spring Hollow culverts. *Paul Collinge, 2016.*

me to Fountain Hughes's Works Project Administration interview. Special thanks to Jim Kauffman, who provided up-to-the-minute photographs of the Blue Ridge Tunnel restoration.

The following members of the Blue Ridge Tunnel Foundation Board of Directors risked life, limb and cellphone accidents to hike mountainous sections of what Claudius Crozet called the "dangerous mile" of Blue Ridge Railroad tracks: Allen Hale, president of the board and an advocate for all my Blue Ridge Tunnel books; Paul Collinge; Bob Dombrowe; and Wayne Nolde. Their intrepid explorations and photography made it possible to annotate maps indicating the general location of slave labor along the line.

Most of the slave labor on the Blue Ridge Railroad occurred in Albemarle County, Virginia. Ann Mallek, member of the Albemarle County Board of Supervisors and a Blue Ridge Tunnel Foundation board member, also encouraged publication of this book. I thank her for recognizing the historical importance of documenting slave labor in Albemarle County.

The presence of Edwina St. Rose at my Blue Ridge Tunnel talk and tour on October 6, 2018, was much appreciated. Her restoration efforts—along with those of many others—at the Daughters of Zion Cemetery made it possible to learn the probable burial place of two enslaved Blue Ridge Railroad laborers.

I thank Arthur Collier for reading two drafts of the text. His encouragement and insightful suggestions gave me heart. Finally, infinite thanks to my husband, Paul Collinge. A superb researcher, he unearthed many of the hidden facts needed for a history of slave labor on the Blue Ridge Railroad.

INTRODUCTION

On August 1, 1818, a commission of twenty-one Virginia state senators convened at the Mountain Top Hotel in Augusta County. The hotel was situated in a windy gap that cuts through the Blue Ridge Mountains mere yards from what is now the intersection of Interstate 64, Skyline Drive and the Blue Ridge Parkway. This spot, including the east and west slopes, was known—and still is—as Rockfish Gap. More commonly, people call it Afton Mountain.

The view from Mountain Top was splendid. Gazing east, members of the commission could see the long descending grade of Rockfish Gap and the distant Southwest Mountains that framed the small town of Charlottesville. The city of Staunton and the Alleghany Mountains were visible to the west. With its cool breezes, Rockfish Gap was a felicitous location for a summer gathering. Moreover, it was a convenient midway point between the eastern Tidewater part of the state and the mountainous western section. Climbing the Blue Ridge from either direction meant an uncomfortable stagecoach journey along rough mountain roads. Commission members split the difference by meeting at Mountain Top.

Former U.S. presidents Thomas Jefferson and James Madison were in attendance. Jefferson authored the first draft of the Declaration of Independence in 1776. Madison was one of seventy men who signed the U.S. Constitution in 1787, and he wrote the Bill of Rights in 1789. The two men, combined, personally enslaved at least seven hundred people, some of whom helped build their respective plantation houses of Monticello in

Center: Rockfish Gap in the Blue Ridge Mountains of Virginia, 2013. *Author's collection.*

Mountain Top Hotel. *John W. Wayland, Stonewall Jackson's Way, 1940.*

eastern Albemarle County and Montpelier in neighboring Orange County. Between 1785 and 1798, hired slave labor helped construct the Jefferson-designed capitol in Richmond. While Jefferson served as secretary of state and then vice president in the 1790s, hired-out enslaved men built the U.S. Capitol in Washington D.C. The former presidents' belief that slave labor was at the disposal of white America was profoundly deep and shared throughout most of the country.[1]

One of the commissioners' tasks was choosing a site for the University of Virginia and its building layout. Thomas Jefferson wanted the university in Charlottesville, where he had already ordered ten slaves to clear fields for a proposed school called Central College. Senators from west of the Blue Ridge hoped the state's first university would be located in Staunton or Lexington, home of Washington College. The eastern senators were in the majority and outvoted them. The university, organized around Jefferson's plan for an academical village, would be in Charlottesville. Five months later, the general assembly agreed.[2]

Leased slave labor was at the heart of the academical village construction. For the next eight years, enslaved men leveled the land, lugged timber and nailed boards. An enslaved stone hauler, one blacksmith and fifteen brickmakers provided additional labor. During the building years of 1820 through 1825, the board of visitors paid $3,780.45 in leasing fees to local slaveholders. When the university welcomed its first forty students, the Rotunda was still under construction, but the pavilions, student residences and boarding hotels were finished.[3]

In 1849, thirty-one years after the commission met, Claudius Crozet—a slaveholding U.S. citizen born in France—spent a week of summer nights at the same Mountain Top Hotel. From its gracious front porch, he observed the pleasing vista with an engineer's mathematical eye. His goal as the state's chief engineer was to survey a railroad line through and over the Blue Ridge at Rockfish Gap, thereby connecting the capital city of Richmond with the Shenandoah Valley. By the 1840s, breaching the Blue Ridge Mountains with a railroad was of supreme importance for Virginia's trade and passenger travel. Yet, despite a statewide clamor from citizens, no private Virginia railroad could raise sufficient funds for the massive task.

That same year, 1849, Virginia's general assembly finally approved state funding for the almost seventeen-mile-long route. Thirteen of those miles—more than three-quarters of the line—were in western Albemarle County, where a dense concentration of the county's enslaved populace toiled.

Rebuilt serpentine wall at the University of Virginia, where archaeologists have discovered an original serpentine wall under a building that housed enslaved people. *Author's collection.*

A glimpse of their lives can be seen in a diary entry written by a visitor who tramped through the Greenwood area in August 1852: "This day was extremely hot….We found seven negroes at work on the side of a hill—three men and four women. They were all ragged and extremely dirty. The men were digging round a rock and the women were shovelling [*sic*] dirt into a cart. One white man was 'overseeing' them. We thought there was some[thing] grand and monarchial in his appearance, as he sat there on a rock overlooking and directing."[4]

The remaining four miles of the railroad crossed corners of Nelson and Augusta Counties. Still in operation, all of the tracks follow, for the most part, the original path that Crozet mapped through the slopes and grassy hills of Rockfish Gap. Continuing the pattern of using hired-out enslaved men for large public projects, the state relied on their labor for the Blue Ridge Railroad. In other words, construction of the University of Virginia and the Blue Ridge Railroad with slave labor, thirty years later, were politically all of a piece.[5]

And physically they were all of a piece. While Claudius Crozet was surveying Rockfish Gap in 1849, Louisa Railroad tracks from Richmond to Charlottesville were still under construction. Then, in early 1850, the general assembly changed the company's name. It would now be the Virginia Central. When the Central, as it was soon called, completed the link in December 1850, travelers from Richmond could finally reach the University of Virginia by rail.[6]

It was the end of a line built, as usual, with slave labor. As the Louisa Railroad Company president wrote, "This work has been undertaken altogether by our citizens employing, as common labourers, their own and the negroes belonging to the country [countryside]."[7]

The next goal was reaching Mechum's River eight miles west of Charlottesville. At that point, the Virginia Central would connect with the future state-funded Blue Ridge Railroad. The railroad bridge over Mechum's River at the intersection of Highways 250 and 240 in western Albemarle marked the eastern beginning of Crozet's project. The South River Bridge in Waynesboro, Virginia, marked the western end. Four tunnels linked the tracks between. Best known is the defunct, almost one-mile-long Blue Ridge Tunnel, where enslaved men labored in 1854, 1855 and 1856. The passage begins in Nelson County and emerges in Augusta County.

The remaining tunnels, Greenwood, Brooksville and Little Rock, connected mountain ridges in western Albemarle. No evidence has been found showing that the state used enslaved men to help build these

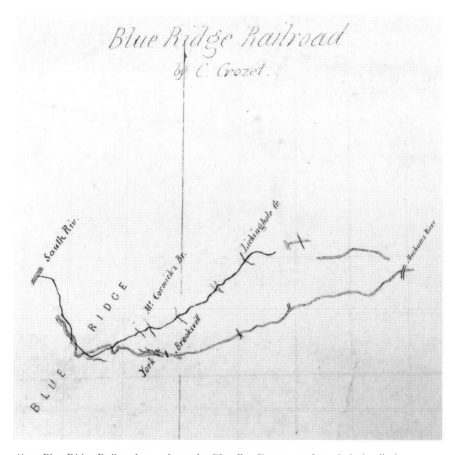

Above: Blue Ridge Railroad map drawn by Claudius Crozet, no date. *Author's collection.*

Opposite, top: Inside the Blue Ridge Tunnel east portal during restoration of the passage in 2019. *Paul Collinge, 2019.*

Opposite, bottom: The four Blue Ridge Railroad tunnels and their lengths. *Green Peyton map 1875, Library of Congress.*

passages, though they labored on every inch of the track beds that ran before, between and beyond.

Only a handful of individual slave records are available for the privately run Louisa and Virginia Central Railroad companies, but a wealth of material exists for the Blue Ridge Railroad because the state saved official documents. Blue Ridge Railroad Papers show that approximately fifteen hundred men and boys built the line. Most were Irish immigrants, recent exiles from the Great Hunger (1845–52) still stalking their homeland.

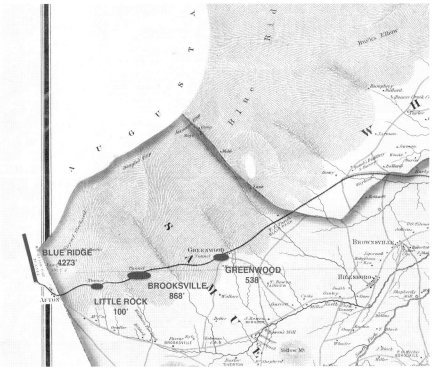

This is to Certify, That C. CROZET, Chief Engineer of the Blue Ridge Rail-road, in obedience to a Resolution adopted by the Board of Public Works of Virginia, on the 10th day of December 1853, has hired of *Robert F. Harris*

for one year from the *1st* day of *January* 185*4* *one* negro man, named

to be employed upon the Work under the charge of the said Chief Engineer; in considera-tion whereof, the said Board of Public Works are to pay to the said *Robert F. Harris* *his* heirs or assigns, *One hundred and fifty* dollars, payable *quarterly* and to furnish the said negro during the year, with the customary Clothing, *Hat & Blanket*

Witness the signature of the said Chief Engineer this *9th* day of *January* 185*4*

Ritchies & Dunnavant, Prs.—Richmond, Va.

Above: Contract between Claudius Crozet and Robert F. Harris for rental of an enslaved man's labor. *Author's collection.*

Opposite, top: Receipt for payment from Claudius Crozet to Robert F. Harris for rental of an enslaved man's labor. *Author's collection.*

Opposite, bottom: Dry brush line: Louisa Railroad 1848–49. Dash line: Virginia Central Railroad 1850–53. Solid line: Blue Ridge Railroad 1850–58. *Green Peyton map 1875, Library of Congress.*

The papers also show that roughly three hundred enslaved men and boys were Blue Ridge Railroad laborers. Financial arrangements for obtaining their labor could take one of three paths. Some slaveholders signed one-year contracts directly with Claudius Crozet during the traditional hiring period at Christmastime. The state paid them quarterly or yearly for each man's work. Alternatively, railroad contractors made individual arrangements to hire slave labor from local slaveholders, paying them—out-of-pocket—with profits earned on the contracted sections. The third route was simple and economical: some Blue Ridge Railroad contractors used people they already held in slavery.[8]

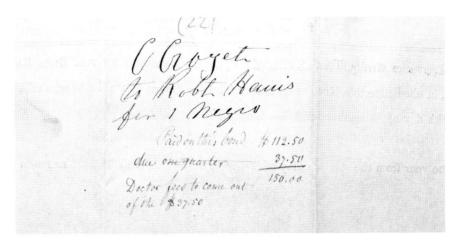

Crozet summarized the first two methods for the Board of Public Works:

> *In order to save time, I have directed Mr. Wm. M. Sclater, who is a good manager, industrious, honest and reliable, to secure hands as soon as he can; and I herewith submit his bid, either as superintendent or contractor; in the first case, the hands would be hired for one year in the name of the Board; in the second, he would hire them upon his own responsibility, and they would cease to be a charge on the day of the completion of the work they have to do.*[9]

The use of slave labor for the University of Virginia in Charlottesville in the early nineteenth century is inextricably bound with the use of slave labor that built the railroad at the university in the mid-nineteenth century. Active tracks still travel through Grounds, as the campus is called. Daily locomotives pull cars that wind through the university hospital complex and clatter over students' heads at the Fourteenth Street and University Avenue intersection. The consist, as train buffs call it, then rolls through honeysuckle thickets growing on both sides of the tracks. It bisects the fraternity area, swoops under Beta Bridge and parallels the Rockfish Gap Turnpike on its journey west to the old Blue Ridge Railroad tracks.

Longtime merchants near the university scarcely notice the rattle of floors and windows in their aging buildings when the locomotives rumble by. "Trains come along every day," says one business owner, "but I don't really remember when." His comment is an innocent yet fitting metaphor for the unheralded, enslaved people who helped build the Louisa, Virginia Central and Blue Ridge Railroads—all part of the same line that increased the wealth of white, antebellum Virginia.[10]

1
1849–50

IN THE HEAT OF THE SUMMER

The first evidence of slave labor on the Blue Ridge Railroad comes from a receipt written to chief engineer Claudius Crozet. It shows his payment for the nine-month hire of Sherrod in 1849. This was the same year that Crozet traversed the slopes of Rockfish Gap as he surveyed a line for the future Blue Ridge Railroad. The chief engineer was somewhat stout and sixty years old. His tools were hefty and cumbersome, yet delicate. It is highly probable that Sherrod, identified as a "boy" on receipts for his room and board, functioned as a pack mule by lugging the instruments for Crozet. Sherrod labored six days a week.[11]

Even with an enslaved porter, crisscrossing miles of rough terrain on horseback was a challenge for the aging Crozet. He soon hired a party of six assistants. In the summer of 1849, they boarded at the Long House, a western Albemarle County inn owned by John S. Cocke.

The following excerpt from Crozet's letter to the Board of Public Works shows that he initially used slave labor for transporting his assistants' surveying tools:

Gentlemen
You will…observe in Mr. Cocke's account an item, which may present itself
as such and requires explanation—From his house, the most convenient to

our work, in the heat of the summer, we had to go occasionally 4 miles to the work, part of it up a steep mountain and the same distance to go over in the evening, with heavy instruments and rods to carry—The fatigue produced by this, would have disabled my assistants from executing as much of the duties of the day we were able to accomplish by hiring a conveyance for them and the instruments—Frequently these are carried by negroes hired by the month for the purpose, but I thought that the hire of a conveyance, when necessary, would answer as well and be cheaper…C. Crozet Eng. B.R.R.R. [12]

Crozet also asked state officials for a raise of his assistants' wages so they could pay their own room and board as they moved along the surveying line. In at least one location, they had the aid of an enslaved person whom the innkeeper referred to as a "servant." Crozet negotiated a discount rate of fifty cents a night for the assistants and twenty-five cents for the so-called servant. Presumably, the lower rate reflected an inferior place for sleeping—a barn, perhaps—and lower quality or quantity of food. [13]

In addition to boarding at Cocke's Long House, the chief engineer maintained various temporary offices on the construction route. West to east, these were the Gibbs Hotel and Mountain Top Hotel in Augusta County; the Mirador, Wallace and Brooksville plantations in western Albemarle County; and Yancey Mills, also in western Albemarle. Wherever Crozet spent the night, enslaved people cared for his horse, prepared and served his meals and laundered his clothes. [14]

Writing from Yancey Mills in December 1849, Claudius Crozet penned a letter to the second auditor for the Board of Public Works. The subject

Receipt to Claudius Crozet for his payment of $102 to rent the labor of Sherrod, an enslaved man. *Author's collection.*

John Cocke's Long House is now a private residence. *Author's collection.*

This Y-level surveying telescope sits on Y-shaped supports. It once belonged to Claudius Crozet and is displayed at the Library of Virginia. *Author's collection.*

Claudius Crozet's 1852 receipt from John Cocke for payment to rent the labor of Ellick, an enslaved man. *Author's collection.*

was culverts, a topic so critical that he mentioned them almost sixty times in his Blue Ridge Railroad correspondence between 1849 and 1858. "The weather favors us," Crozet cheerily announced. "M. Sizer is building his shanties—his three sections are staked out. Laying of walls, abutments of culverts etc which are our next work, will come after frost and then keep us pretty busy. Ever your friend, C. Crozet."[15]

That same month, the chief engineer designated construction of the Blue Ridge Railroad on the east side of Rockfish Gap as sections one through eight. Section one was the Blue Ridge Tunnel, including one thousand feet beyond the planned approaches to each portal. Section two began at a long outcropping of rock visible on the current Nelson County greenway to the Blue Ridge Tunnel east portal. Section three headed east through a hilly landscape in Albemarle County. Section four ended just east of what is now Little Rock Tunnel. Sections five and six included the Brooksville and Greenwood Tunnels. Irish immigrants and local white laborers built these latter passages.[16]

The combined length of sections two, three and four was almost sixteen thousand feet or about three miles. When Mordecai Sizer, a former James River Canal contractor from King William County, bid for them, he presented a recommendation letter. "Mordecai Sizer is an efficient contractor," it stated, "and has now at his command a considerable black force."[17]

The guarantee of slave labor must have appealed to Crozet and the Board of Public Works; out of sixteen bids, they accepted Sizer's for the three sections. The first contractor to break ground on the railroad project, Sizer began with a mixed-race force of Irish immigrants, local men and as many as 72 enslaved laborers—145 hands in all. Both Sizer and Crozet boarded at the Brooksville Inn located in western Albemarle County and owned by planter George Farrow. Sizer was residing there when the 1850 federal census taker listed him on the slave schedule as holding 37 enslaved

Little Rock Tunnel is the only one of the four Blue Ridge Railroad tunnels still in operation. *Allen Hale, 2016.*

males. All but 4 were old enough for work on the railroad, including a ten-year-old boy. Sizer likely hired local slave labor to supplement the 37 people he brought to Albemarle.[18]

As seen in Crozet's December 1849 letter, Sizer first directed his force to build shanties. The men would have fashioned them from timber they felled in the railroad's right of way. The structures, squeezed between a hill and the future track bed, were surely overcrowded and substandard. As one Virginia slave agent wrote, "There is a great difference between hard work, through cold & hot wet & dry & living under a shantee and being provided with good lodging & kep'd in the house in bad wether [*sic*]."[19]

Now that Sizer's crew members had flimsy roofs over their heads, their culvert labor could begin. Culverts were curved or square enclosures constructed with rock, cement, brick or a combination. When completed, they resembled miniature tunnels and channeled rainwater coursing down mountain slopes along the line. Man-made embankments thirty to eighty feet high and up to two hundred feet long covered the culverts. Only when the men finished this labor-intensive understructure could railroad tracks be laid on top. Crozet chose the culvert locations by January 1850. For the next nine months, construction of smaller culverts progressed well on Sizer's stretch. "On the 2d, 3d, and 4th sections," Crozet reported in October 1850, "6,000 feet (say 1¼ mile) are nearly completed besides many considerable culverts."[20]

But not all was going well. "One of the greatest difficulties experienced on this work," Crozet told the Board of Public Works, "has been the want of building stone…for the construction of retaining walls and the numerous culverts which pass under the [rail]road, we have had nothing but slate rock to depend on."[21]

Though slate was tolerable for small culverts, the need for harder stone was acute at three creases on the eastern slope of Rockfish Gap. Crozet defined this area as "probably the most difficult and expensive mile…we have to cross three deep hollows in succession." West to east, these were the Goodloe and Robertson Hollows, followed by Dove Spring Hollow on section five. In these three hollows, he wrote, "Most of the frequent ravines, which furrow the face of the mountain, discharge at times large volumes of water."[22]

Mordecai Sizer's sections three and four included Goodloe and Robertson Hollows. It was here that his enslaved force had their most demanding labor. "On the 3rd & 4th sections, two large culverts have to be built," Crozet wrote, "the principal one under the high bank across Robertson's hollow; after

Robertson Hollow culverts. *Paul Collinge, 2016.*

having, in vain, searched the whole neighbourhood for suitable materials, I have concluded that it would be expedient to construct these culverts with limestone, though hauled a distance from 8 to 10 miles."[23]

Initially, Crozet controlled the flow of creeks gushing down the two slopes by filling them with rocks, creating a kind of French drain. But he worried that leaves and sediment would choke the waterways during spring torrents, causing them to flood the embankment and destabilize tracks that would eventually run on top. Anticipating blockage, he eventually called for a quadruplet of nearly two-hundred-foot-long box culverts to be built at Robertson Hollow and a pair of the same at Goodloe Hollow.[24]

Crozet composed twelve specifications for building culverts. One of them stated:

> *Box or rectangular culverts, single or double, whether covered or open. Such culverts will be built dry, unless otherwise directed, and of hard sound stone. They shall nowhere be less than eighteen inches, nor more than 2½ (two and a half) feet wide. Where the foundation is not solid, they will be paved within the abutments with stones set on edge, breaking*

joints with an apron wall of suitable depth, and about one foot thick at each end. The thickness of the abutments shall be at least ⅔ (two thirds) of their height, and in no case less than 2 (two) feet. They shall be built according to the general directions for dry walls, except as regards the size of the stones, the beds of which may be reduced to a minimum thickness of six inches, the stones being at least twelve inches wide, with a header to two stretchers; the headers to extend at least one foot back of the stretchers. The covering stones to be strong and durable, at least six inches thick, and resting on the abutments not less than nine inches. The thickness of the aggregate top not less than one foot. Suitable wings will be added when judged expedient by the engineer.[25]

Mordecai Sizer definitely used slave labor to execute the chief engineer's precise instructions, but determining exactly who on his mixed-race crew did what is impossible now. For constructing culverts, enslaved men skilled at rock cutting and stone masonry would have been a valuable component of the group, whereas the unskilled men were informal apprentices who learned by watching and supervised practice.[26]

Double culverts at Goodloe Hollow. The vertical yardstick between them indicates height. *Paul Collinge, 2015.*

A PREJUDICE AGAINST RAILROADS

As Sizer's crew struggled with the challenging box culverts at Robertson and Goodloe Hollows, progress on sections seven and eight of the Blue Ridge Railroad was more encouraging. This flatter portion of the line began east of what would be Greenwood Tunnel and ended at Blair Park plantation, west of the present-day town of Crozet. The signer of Claudius Crozet's contract for sections seven and eight was Thomas Jefferson Randolph. The oldest grandson of Thomas Jefferson, Randolph was a member of the University of Virginia's Board of Visitors from 1829 to 1853 and was later the rector.[27]

Randolph and the enslaved crew under his control were no strangers to culverts. In 1848 and 1849, his force built at least three for the Louisa Railroad near his Edgehill plantation at Shadwell in eastern Albemarle County. The culverts required strong backs and, as always, a handy supply of rock. "Pa's railroad work, is coming on bravely," wrote one of Randolph's

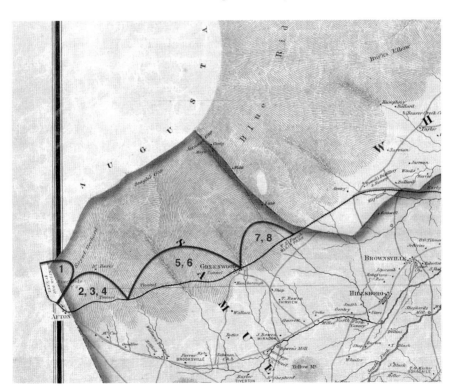

Sections one through eight. Section one included the Blue Ridge Tunnel and its approaches. *Green Peyton map 1875, Library of Congress.*

Culvert that enslaved men built at Shadwell for Thomas Jefferson Randolph's contract on the Louisa Railroad, circa 1848–49. *Paul Collinge, 2019.*

daughters to her sister while she and her father were in Richmond. "Tell him that Culvert No 3 is not much more than half done, and I dont think they have nearly enough stone for it, where they will get rocks five feet long to cover it is more than I can tell."[28]

Center right: Slave schedule for Thomas Jefferson Randolph and Christopher Valentine, 1850, page one of two. *National Archives.*

For his Louisa Railroad contract, Randolph could access the enslaved population at Edgehill, hired-out men from the surrounding countryside or both. But Christopher Valentine, his silent partner on the Blue Ridge Railroad, had difficulty finding enough laborers for sections seven and eight. "I think there is a prejudice in this neighburhood [*sic*] against Railroads with both Masters and hands," he wrote to Randolph from Louisa County in late 1849, "and possibly we may do better in your neighbourhood than we can here."[29]

The reluctance of area slaveholders to hire out slave labor for railroad work meant that Valentine and Randolph began section eight with a minimal crew in April 1850. It included one overseer, eight or nine quarry men (race

Riprap at Little Ivy Creek in western Albemarle County, Virginia. The twelve-inch ruler indicates the size of the rocks. *Author's collection.*

unstated) and twenty-seven "negroes," as Crozet wrote, with five carts. He explained to the Board of Public Works that Randolph's force was "much too small; I have asked him to increase it; but as he works negroes altogether he cannot very conveniently do so."[30]

The twenty-seven enslaved people were very likely part of the same group of thirty-two that Randolph and Valentine jointly hired in 1850, as shown on the federal slave schedule taken in August of that year. Absence of names makes certainty impossible, yet the numbers perfectly match. The twenty-seven men and boys were between ten and forty-five-years old—a common age span for Blue Ridge Railroad laborers. The schedule also listed one enslaved woman—likely a cook and washerwoman for the crew—and four young children, for a total of the slave schedule's figure of thirty-two. Their quarters were located near the railroad on sections seven or eight, as was lodging for Valentine and his family.[31]

The men's labor first entailed chopping down trees on a strip more than sixty feet wide and 2.7 miles long. Their efforts cleared a path for the future track bed and thirty feet of right of way on both sides. Grubbing—digging and pulling out—stumps and other growth followed. Shoveled excavation sufficient to create a level track bed came next. Filling ravines and hauling rock for riprap as an embankment stabilizer were additional tasks. Crozet's specification for riprap was exacting. He wrote that it "shall be of hard durable stone, arranged compactly with the larger and more durable stone outside, with as even a finish as can be made without hammering, and of a thickness to be fixed by the engineer, but nowhere less than one foot." In short, Randolph's enslaved force became human bulldozers, backhoes and jackhammers on a ribbon of land totaling more than nineteen acres.[32]

2

1851–52

THE FORCE EMPLOYED

By April 1851, fifty-one enslaved men and boys were laboring for Thomas Jefferson Randolph on sections seven and eight. Their essential diet and form of labor are evident in Christopher Valentine's progress report in May of that year. He stated that he had received from Scottsville (via the James River Canal) "100 kegs powder, 2 boxes fuses, the steel iron hammers, bacon."[33]

The crew was nearly out of bacon by September. They were also out of fuse, which offers a valuable clue about demands made of them. Though Randolph's sections were fairly level, they called for slicing several deep cuts through the mountainside. It appears that he and Valentine directed the men to pound narrow, tube-shaped holes in the rock, load them with volatile gunpowder and blast the cuts. In those pre-dynamite times, such work demanded steady hands and nerve.[34]

Randolph's contract stipulated that he complete sections seven and eight by January 1, 1854. But, as the end of 1852 approached, his assigned assistant engineer concluded that all the work, including ballast, could be finished that year if Randolph increased his force with state-hired enslaved men. Claudius Crozet agreed. The engineers had good reason to hurry along the job. Ballast on Randolph's sections would create a permanent road sooner than later for westbound trains from the future Mechum's River Depot to Greenwood Tunnel—a passage that was well underway.[35]

Above: The original site of the Mechum's River Depot is now a mulch business. *Bob Dombrowe, 2019.*

Left: Brick abutments at the now-bypassed Greenwood Tunnel. The outer abutment was added sometime after the Blue Ridge Railroad opened. *Library of Congress.*

Christopher Valentine resisted the idea. His enslaved crew ran horses and carts in both directions to transport construction materials along the track bed. State-hired enslaved men laying ballast would slow them down. Valentine consulted with Randolph, who later complained, "The proposition was disadvantageous to us as the state gave a higher price for the hands than we could afford."[36]

Plus, Randolph was committed to area slaveholders for the yearly feeding and clothing of hired-out men already in his force. If they finished sections seven and eight weeks before Christmas, he would be paying for idle laborers—anathema to all Blue Ridge Railroad contractors. He and Valentine grudgingly agreed to the proposal with one provision: "Employment should be given to our hands," Randolph later recalled, "for the balance of the year if the work was completed before Christmas."[37]

By Christmas, sections seven and eight were finished. The bid that Randolph submitted for them in 1849 was $53,558—well over $1.5 million in 2019 dollars. The final amount he charged in 1852, and how much was profit, is unknown. It is highly unlikely that any of his enslaved force or the added state-hired men received a portion of this money for their arduous tasks, though early completion of the work meant one less headache for Claudius Crozet as he struggled with a crisis: The contractor for sections two, three and four no longer wanted the job.[38]

DEBTS INCURRED FOR THE HIRE OF NEGROES

Mordecai Sizer had good reason to leave his Blue Ridge Railroad work in August 1852. Repeated earth slides on his embankments were all too frequent. Crozet described them as "very singular and difficult to account for, though the rock had been bared and left a smooth ledge sloping at an angle in which clay itself would have stood, the whole stratum broke into immense fragments which slid down into the cut and almost filled it."

We can only imagine what Sizer's enslaved crewmembers thought of the slides. They had hand dug the cuts, only to see them collapse and need another round of excavation. Whether or not the men and boys cared about their wasted efforts, they suffered aching muscle pain every day.[39]

Sizer likely took the thirty-seven people he held in slavery with him when he left the area. Any agreements for hired men who made up the balance of his enslaved force may have transferred to the contractors who took over

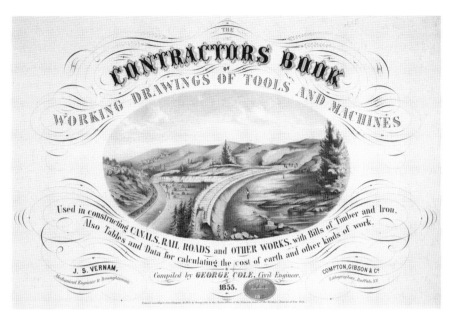

Left: Canal-building scene. *Right*: Railroad-building scene. Every Blue Ridge Railroad contractor probably owned a copy of this popular book. *Library of Congress.*

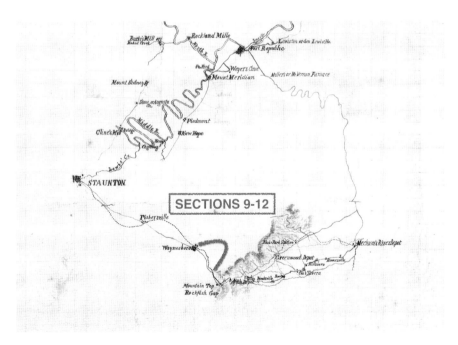

Sections nine through twelve of the Blue Ridge Railroad. *Jedediah Hotchkiss map 1860, Library of Congress.*

his sections in August 1852. George Farrow assumed sections two and three, while section four went to Augusta County contractors Hugh Gallaher and Samuel McElroy.[40]

As a contractor for the James River Canal in 1850, Gallaher was well accustomed to slave labor. And with a different partner, R.L. Walker, he had already used slave labor to build Blue Ridge Railroad sections nine, ten and eleven in Augusta County in 1851. Nine began at the end of the blasted approach to the west portal of the Blue Ridge Tunnel. Ten and eleven continued down the west slope. Twelve included a bridge over the South River at the bottom of the mountain.

Gallaher and Walker's use of slave labor on these sections is evident in the following letter:

> *Richmond December 12ᵗʰ/51*
> *To the Board of Public Works*
> *The undersigned respectfully represent that considerable debts contracted by us in executing the work on the 9 10 11 sections & bridge on the Blue Ridge Rail Road are pressing upon us and that we find it impossible to pay them without assistance from the Board. These debts were incurred for the hire of negroes and for loans from the banks for the payment of current expenses on the work…*
> *Respectfully your obedient servants*
> *R L Walker & H L Gallaher*[41]

Gallaher and Walker paid white laborers $1.00 a day and the enslavers of hired-out laborers from $125.00 to $130.00 a year for the labor of each man. Presumably, they slept in segregated shanties. Board for each enslaved man was $0.70 a week. The clothing allowance for them was $20.00 a year, with an additional dollar per man for a doctor if needed. Similar charges would have accrued for enslaved crews laboring at the Little Rock Tunnel on Gallaher's and McElroy's section four, where the rock was so hard that a single two-foot-deep hole could wear out thirty to forty steel drills.[42]

As to George Farrow's inherited sections two and three, forty-one enslaved people lived on his Brooksville plantation in Greenwood, Virginia. Seventeen were men and boys old enough to labor on his sections in 1852. Farrow lasted only six months. In February 1853, he transferred his contract to Robert P. Smith, a neighboring planter in Greenwood. The reason is unclear.[43]

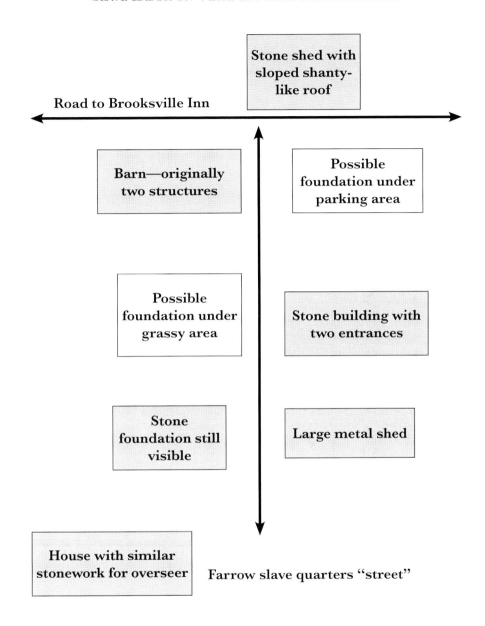

Survey of a Brooksville plantation "street" with ground penetrating radar in 2012 indicated possible building foundations. The structures may have housed enslaved people. *Author's collection.*

Maybe Farrow was already stirring too many Blue Ridge Railroad puddings. Proprietor of the Brooksville Inn, he was also a vendor who provided—for a price—supplies such as oats and sand for the railroad construction. Additionally, Brooksville plantation included five hundred farmable acres where enslaved field hands raised more than two thousand bushels of wheat, corn and oats and hundreds of cattle and sheep. Transactions related to the crops and animals would have needed his input.[44]

Whatever the case, George Farrow's timing for his departure as a contractor turned out to be fortunate for him. Soon after Robert P. Smith took over Farrow's contract for sections two and three in February 1853, all hell broke loose on the Blue Ridge Railroad. James Williams, an enslaved twelve-year-old, would be in the middle of it.

3

1853

RENTED LIKE A HORSE

Two major events threw Blue Ridge Railroad construction into disarray in spring 1853. Greenwood Tunnel was only six months from completion, but treacherous cave-ins and earth slides at the Blue Ridge and Brooksville Tunnels put those borings well behind schedule. Directors of the Virginia Central Railroad, who would take control of Blue Ridge Railroad sections as the state finished them, were distressed by the loss of unrealized freight and passenger monies. They hired Charles Ellet, a bridge engineer, to analyze the problem.[45]

Ellet contended that the Virginia Central must build a temporary track around the incomplete tunnels as soon as possible. He also insisted that the Blue Ridge Railroad finalize its track beds. These tracks would then join with alternating Virginia Central temporary tracks. When the temporary railroad opened, passenger, light freight and mail trains could run the 145 miles from Richmond, through Charlottesville, over Rockfish Gap and all the way to Bath County—the western end of then-finished tracks on the Virginia Central line.[46]

Construction of the temporary track created a labor shortage on every section of the Blue Ridge Railroad. Complicating matters, two Irish laborers died in April—one from a "hurt on the railroad" and the other from an "accidental sliding of earth," according to death records. As a result, some dissatisfied Irish left for work elsewhere, and most of the

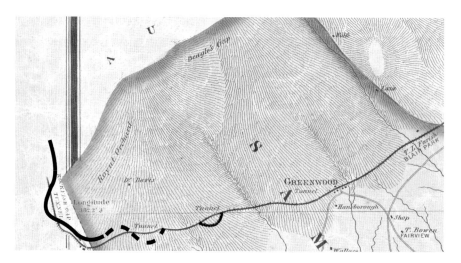

Temporary track. Dry brush line: ½ mile. Dash line: ¾ mile. Solid line: 4.4 miles. *Green Peyton map 1875, Library of Congress.*

remaining men went on a three-week strike for higher wages. Mid-strike, Crozet placed a flurry of advertisements for new Irish recruits in local and big-city eastern newspapers.[47]

Crozet's efforts at finding strikebreakers were unsuccessful. The walkout ended with a compromise pay raise, but he hoped he could avoid further Irish unrest with more hired-out enslaved men and boys. One of them was James Williams.[48]

Williams was born on Thomas Jarman's plantation on August 28, 1840. The estate was located on Jarman's Gap Road about one half mile north of the railroad construction in Albemarle County. Williams never knew his father and so adopted the surname of one of his grandfathers. According to Williams, his enslaved mother was "strong and healthy...she did as much work in the fields as any man. She often carried the 3-horse plow she used upon her shoulders to the implement shed in the evenings after work was done." The mother's labor pains began while she was cutting oats in one of Jarman's fields. Williams recalled that after she gave birth, she "put me in her apron and walked to Thomas Jarman's house."[49]

Thomas Jarman held sixteen people in slavery in 1850. At some point, he gave James Williams to his grown son, William Pleasant Jarman. Due to a perceived disobedience, Williams angered "Marse Billy," as Williams called the younger Jarman. When "Marse Billy" secretly sold James Williams to a Shenandoah Valley planter, Thomas Jarman made his son reverse the sale and bring Williams home.[50]

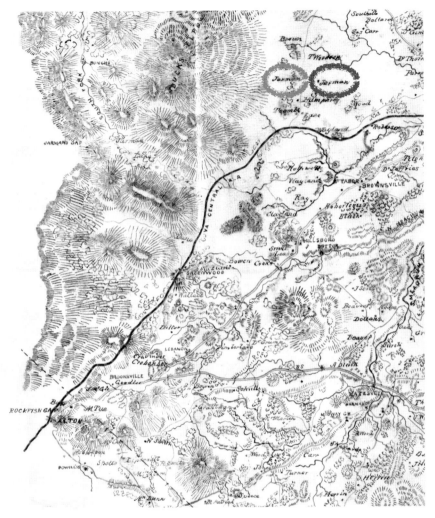

Light gray oval: Thomas Jarman's house. Dark gray oval: An earlier Jarman house. Black line: Railroad. *Albert Campbell map 1864, Library of Congress.*

It seems that both Jarmans controlled James Williams, so we cannot know which one leased his labor to the Blue Ridge Railroad in 1853. Only twelve years old at the time, he recalled later that enslaved people were "rented like a horse." We can assume the Jarmans hired him out for the year.[51]

Williams's recollection of contractor "Bob Smith," as he remembered Robert P. Smith, tells us that the youngster toiled on section two and possibly the much rougher ground of section three. The track bed on section two needed ties and rails when Smith assumed George Farrow's contract. But

Thomas Jarman's house after 1994 and 2008 renovations. *John Armstrong, 2007.*

first, the sloped bed wanted trimming (smoothing), and it lacked ballast on both sides. Explosions on the east side of the Blue Ridge Tunnel provided rock debris for the ballast.[52]

Claudius Crozet's instructions for ballast were detailed: "The ballasting, whether reserved from the excavation or procured independently, must be free from any admixture of clay; the stones not to be larger than cubes of 2 (two) inches. The thickness of the layer to be in general 12 (twelve) inches, except in the tunnels, where it may be reduced to 9, (nine,) and beaten to the requisite depth into a firm and solid mass."[53]

As a cart boy, James Williams would have rolled his wheelbarrow inside the tunnel, loaded it with rock and then hauled and emptied it somewhere along the 5,250 feet of section two. Decades later, he recalled that he helped build the Blue Ridge Tunnel, but Robert P. Smith had no contractual connection whatsoever with the passage. If the boy labored on section two, his access to the tunnel may account for the mistaken recollection.[54]

On section three, Smith continued widening a sixty-four-foot-high embankment at Goodloe Hollow. When it was stable and level on top, his force could then create the track bed. Rock for the Goodloe embankment

Ballasted tracks on top of the man-made Goodloe Hollow embankment. *Paul Collinge, 2006.*

CSX train exiting the west portal of Little Rock Tunnel. *Paul Collinge, 2016.*

came from explosions at the adjacent one-hundred-foot-long Little Rock Tunnel. This passage, begun in 1853—the same year the Jarmans hired out James Williams—marked the eastern end of section three. Williams would have carted rocks from the Little Rock Tunnel on section four and unloaded them somewhere along section three. If the young fellow labored on section three, perhaps he remembered the Little Rock Tunnel as the Blue Ridge Tunnel.[55]

We have no way of knowing if James Williams toiled on section two, three or both. No matter, Robert P. Smith used Williams as a dump truck during the frantic months of preparation for the temporary track. The boy would have wheeled the cart six days a week, sunup to sundown. Blue Ridge Railroad pay for Irish boys under the approximate age of sixteen ranged from $0.54½ to $0.75 a day in 1853. Irish wages often set the rate for hired slave labor; the state likely paid the Jarmans a similar amount for the labor of Williams.[56]

The severe labor shortage of 1853 affected Virginia Central contractors, as well. It also presented Robert P. Smith an opportunity for additional profit from hired slave labor. Both can be seen in Claudius Crozet's letter to the Board of Public Works:

> *That hands are very scare* [scarce] *is a widely known fact, and more strikes may be shortly expected. Mr. C.R. Mason, as honest a man as there is in Christendom, and who is extensively employed by the Central r.r. co., assures me that that company is greatly in want of hands; he himself is now engaged on the temporary track over the Blue ridge, and has only 50 hands with him; he is trying every thing to get additions, but without, so far, any success: Mr. Ellett* [sic] *himself has gone to the north to get some, and I have authorized him to get a number also for me. A gentleman, Mr. Rob. P. Smith, assures me that he can get me a force of 50 or 60 negroes to work at the* [Blue Ridge] *Tunnel, if I will allow him for them Irish wages, and insure them employment for the year of their hire, which I have promised, subject to your ratification—He is to be in town* [Richmond] *tomorrow, and will lay the matter before you.*[57]

So serious was the 1853 labor shortage that the Virginia Central and Blue Ridge Railroad contractors borrowed enslaved people from one another on occasion. For example, Blue Ridge Railroad hired-out men who toiled on section three near the Little Rock Tunnel also labored for Claiborne Rice Mason on the Virginia Central's adjacent temporary track. "I came to Smith's work, whose hands were idle," Crozet wrote, "we thought they had been taking their breakfast, but when we returned from the new Tunnel [Little Rock], they were gone.—we then overtook a black boy and asked him whom he belonged to; his answer was 'to Mr. Smith.' Where are you going to?—to Mr. Mason's work.—where are the other boys?—at work with Mr. Mason."[58]

Meanwhile, still more slave labor was used to prepare section four for the future temporary railroad. Embankments needed stabilizing, and repairs were required on two-year-old culverts at Robertson Hollow. The force for Gallaher and McElroy, who inherited Sizer's section four, reinforced the culverts with cement in 1853. The contractors' expenditure for hired slave labor is obvious from a letter their financial backer sent to the board:[59]

Augusta Co. Dec 3. 1853
To the Board of P. Works.
Richmond Va.
Gentlemen having a lien on the reservation money of R.L. Walker Co. &
Galaher [sic] & McElroy I hereby relinquish it to as much as the Board
may think proper to advance to them as they are anxious to get an advance
for the purpose of paying their hire of Negroes.
Respectfully
Sam B. Brown

Robertson Hollow culverts. The man-made embankment over them is about eighty feet high. *Allen Hale, 2016.*

SECTION SIXTEEN

Sections thirteen through fifteen on the west side of Rockfish Gap lay between Waynesboro and Staunton in Augusta County. The Virginia Central Railroad raised most of the money for this stretch of the line, while the state contributed a small amount. As chief engineer of the Blue Ridge Railroad, Crozet numbered these sections and executed the contracts in 1851 and 1852. Slave labor was used on all three sections.[60]

In 1852, Crozet numbered section sixteen. Eight miles long, it was located between Mechum's River and Blair Park plantation on the east side of Rockfish Gap. Pressure to finalize all culvert work on the Blue Ridge Railroad increased greatly with the coming of the temporary track. Eleven contractors in all were involved with section sixteen and what Claudius Crozet described as its difficult "lower extremity" at Lickinghole Creek, which called for a particularly challenging culvert. Only four fulfilled their commitments; the others were replaced. This whiplash of successive contractors meant a frequent change of overseers. For survival, the enslaved crews quickly had to discern their new bosses' moods and methods of enforcement. And the constant change of location and tasks would have placed an extra burden on the older, less physically agile men.[61]

Clement L. Lukins, who likely employed an Irish force, was the first contractor to abandon section sixteen. Using a mixed-race crew, Hugh Gallaher and Samuel McElroy assumed Lukins's contract in December 1852. Four months later, they turned it over to William M. Sclater. Sclater used only enslaved men or "gangs," as Claudius Crozet called them.[62]

William S. Carter of Louisa County was also contracted for parts of section sixteen. He had already used hired slave labor on sections thirteen and fourteen west of Waynesboro. He then transferred the men to ballast track beds on section sixteen. Their backbreaking tasks are apparent in Claudius Crozet's explanation to the Board of Public Works: "Mssrs Carter & Gooch will both soon complete their contracts and having a number of negroes hired for the year, they have proposed to have them thus employed....In some places, the ground will require no ballasting, in others the stone will be obtained on the spot out of cuts, in some cases it will have to be got out of quarries and hauled a long distance."[63]

Carter's time on section sixteen was brief. When Virginia's attorney general advised the Board of Public Works that the contractor was guilty of fraud by charging double for cart drivers, Carter abruptly abandoned the work, leaving all tools and implements behind. His successor was Robert P. Smith.[64]

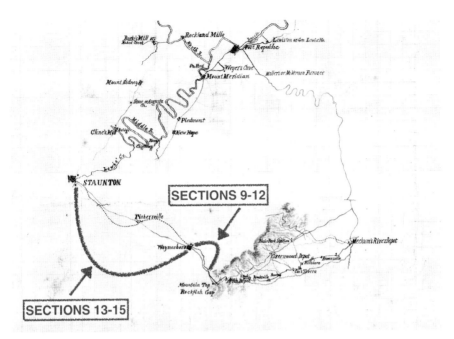

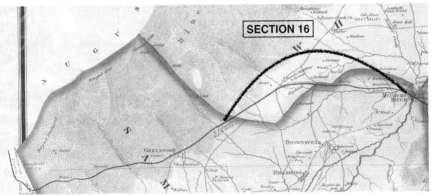

Top: Sections nine through fifteen of the Blue Ridge Railroad. *Jedediah Hotchkiss map 1860, Library of Congress.*

Bottom: Section sixteen of the Blue Ridge Railroad. *Green Peyton map 1875, Library of Congress.*

Smith's section sixteen contract stated he would engage "as large a force as can be employed to advantage" for "all the work that may be judged necessary." Two members of his crew were white foremen. The remaining men were enslaved, including Phil, a blacksmith whose rate of pay was $37.50 a month. Using tools that he forged and sharpened, the laborers smoothed the top and sides of the track bed. They shored up embankments, removed earth slides, cleared flooded ditches and distributed crossties that the Blue Ridge Railroad purchased from Smith. The men's tasks included ballasting. As Claudius Crozet described it, "1,800 cubic yards of ballasting per mile, to be procured, broken, spread, and rammed in."[65]

Despite progress along section sixteen, the Lickinghole Creek culvert remained unfinished. Claudius Crozet hired two local men to solve the problem: W.B. Phillips, a bricklayer, and John R. Holmes, a stonemason. Phillips held thirty-seven people in slavery in 1850. Thirteen of them were old enough for railroad work. Some or all may have built the demanding culvert. In any case, Phillips and Holmes purchased fuse for gunpowder blasting—an indication of the great struggle at Lickinghole Creek.[66]

Laborers removed supports from the large arch on the Lickinghole Creek culvert in June 1853, and Crozet could finally tell the board that the structure was done. The men raised the forty-five-foot-high embankment over the culvert by August and then repaired a small box culvert in December. Now the laying of rails on section sixteen could proceed, as Crozet stated, "to accommodate as speedily as possible the traveling public."[67]

ECONOMY OF PROGRESS

Finding enslaved people such as James Williams for "contingent" work, as Claudius Crozet termed the trimming and ballasting of tracks, was easy enough. Deciding on slave labor for the more dangerous Blue Ridge Tunnel construction was another matter. Memories of the three-week Irish strike in April 1853 were fresh in Crozet's mind when he suggested that the state directly hire one hundred enslaved laborers for the tunnel in the coming year of 1854. During the strike, Irish hands had refused to let anyone operate the horse-driven pumps, leaving the west side of the tunnel filled with water that gushed from fissures in the sides and roof of the passage. After returning to work, the Irish wasted days draining it. If they walked off the job again, thought Crozet, an enslaved crew could man the pumps until the strike ended.[68]

"Should the Board determine upon this plan," Crozet advised, "a general Superintendent of this force and a number of foremen must also be engaged, to direct and protect them. This being the hiring Season, I would suggest that instructions be given to a proper agent to proceed at

A spring rain flooding the east portal of the Blue Ridge Tunnel. *Jim Kauffman, 2015.*

once in this business, and to select, as much as possible, such men as have been employed in coal pits."[69]

Equally important to Claudius Crozet, black men running the pumps would be physically separate from white men who drilled and blasted deep in the mountain. Crozet's fears about mixing races in the Blue Ridge Tunnel

BLUE RIDGE TUNNEL
COLLATERAL OPERATIONS:

Floorer
Stonecutter
Carpenter
Blacksmith
Ostler
Smith helper
At pump
Dumper
Waterman
At quarry
Mason
Mason's apprentice
Crank
Tool carrier[*]

were based on conflicts at other southern railroads but were unfounded for this project. Considering the time pressure caused by the temporary railroad, his advice for hiring slave labor by the end of the year appeared sound to the board, and it approved the decision:[70] "Resolved, that the chief engineer of the Blue Ridge Railroad, be and he is hereby authorized to have as many negroes as can be profitably employed on the work under his charge, and to make such arrangements, therefor [*sic*], as may be necessary."[71]

Crozet first consulted Toler and Cook, a Richmond business that specialized in renting slave labor. George W. Toler and John R. Cook operated from a "stand," as Cook called it, under Metropolitan Hall in the heart of the city's slave trade district. Crozet's hopes surely sank when he learned from Toler and Cook that "masters, generally, object to hiring for the Tunnel...only a few negroes were mentioned as likely to be obtained at a price of $200 [per year]."[72]

Meanwhile, William Sclater, one of the section sixteen contractors, scoured the region for willing enslavers. None would agree to rent out laborers for the Blue Ridge Tunnel to him or to Robert P. Smith. Pushed for time as the hiring season closed, Crozet must have been relieved when George Farrow, his temporary landlord at Brooksville Inn, agreed that he and his brother-in-law, David Hansbrough, would rent the labor of "40 to 50 negroes," as Crozet reported. He wrote that they would be "hired by the day, to work in the tunnel at every collateral operation, but not to be employed in blasting."[73] (See appendix 1.)

Though George Farrow charged a higher pay rate than Crozet wanted—$1.12½ a day, based on better wages the Irish had achieved with their three-week strike—slave labor in the Blue Ridge Tunnel was a victory for the chief engineer. "Fifty negroes in the tunnel will relieve the white hands," he reminded the board, "and enable us to have a full force at the drills, thus producing virtually an economy in the way of progress."[74]

[*]Blue Ridge Railroad payrolls, 1854–57, BRP.

4

1854

MASTERS OF THEIR MASTERS

The Blue Ridge Tunnel was "long, smoky, and wet," said John Larguey, one of the native-born Irish contractors in charge of building it. A degree of daylight penetrated the east portal in the morning and the west portal in the afternoon. But the headings, as they advanced deeper toward the center of the almost one-mile-long bore, were lit only with lanterns and were in perpetual twilight. Though Crozet used pumps, the men and boys were often wet to the skin. Some of the water, he observed, "fell from the roof as a heavy summer shower."[75]

Crozet further noted that "smoke was very troublesome," especially during hot, still August weather. Inhaling air thick with silica-laden dust after rock blasts would have caused labored breathing. Making matters worse, the passage, by now eighteen hundred feet long, stank. A visitor described the odor: "The first thing we encountered was the smell of gun powder—not like powder that has just been burnt but an old-strong-sour-wet smell peculiarly sickening."[76]

Plus, round-the-clock explosions made the tunnel deafeningly noisy. That same visitor spent the night in a place he termed the "tunnel house." It was near the west portal. "We were wet, tired and sleepy, and went to bed," he wrote in his diary. "In the night we were startled by the blasting of rocks in the belly of the mountain. Peal after peal—'louder than the bolts of

Moss, paint and eighty-eight years of soot inside the Blue Ridge Tunnel west portal. *Paul Collinge, 2019.*

Heaven' it seemed to shake the whole Blue Ridge, and jarred the house till the windows rattled in their frames."[77]

No wonder ten of the enslaved men who arrived at the tunnel on Monday, January 9, fled the sorry worksite. Some who labored that day were gone by February. Crozet's dismay was evident in his letter to the Board of Public Works: "Messrs. Farrow & Hansbrough," he complained, "failed to procure the requisite number of negroes, they had obtained 33, but, when brought to the tunnel, 10 of them ran away and were withdrawn by their masters: for, at present, in hiring, it appears that negroes have become masters of their masters. Those who remain work well and are satisfied: I hope they will induce others to join them."[78]

Blue Ridge Tunnel payroll with names of enslaved men, January 1854. A notation on the page states, "This list contains none but negroes." *Author's collection.*

Apparently, a few of the runaways returned, or a second, different group of men were ordered to the passage. A total of thirty-one enslaved men ended up at the Blue Ridge Tunnel in 1854 but not all at the same time. Overseer William Ramsay enslaved two of the laborers. George Farrow and David Hansbrough personally enslaved or hired additional, local slave labor, for a combined total of twenty-nine men. At least two sets of the enslaved laborers were related. Wesley Carter, held by Hansbrough, and Samuel Carter, enslaved by Farrow, may have been brothers. Albert and Lewis Hartshorn, also held by Farrow, were probably kinsmen.[79]

Abraham, Robert Mickums and Thomas Barns were master blacksmiths at the Blue Ridge Tunnel. Likely, their sheds were located just outside the east portal. They brought in $1.40 a day each for the slaveholders that year. Assigned tasks for the rest of the group are uncertain. For one month, all of them toiled as floorers, clearing rubble after blasts. But Claudius Crozet's plan for an enslaved crew that would operate pumps on the west side of the tunnel came to nothing. Payrolls show that all of the enslaved men labored exclusively on the east side.[80]

Where the men slept at night is an open question. David Hansbrough owned Nelson County land very near the Blue Ridge Tunnel east portal, and George Farrow's Brooksville plantation was only three downhill miles east of it. It makes sense that the enslaved tunnel laborers would have left their plantation quarters and traveled by wagon up to the passage at dawn, returning the same way at dusk for their usual victuals and pallet beds. (Ann Goodloe's house and land were adjacent to those of George Farrow. She enslaved Samuel Carter's wife, Rhoda, and the couple's eleven offspring. Farrow may have allowed Carter a nightly return to his wife and children at the Goodloe plantation.)[81]

Additionally, scores of Irish were living in shanties along the steep, narrow ravine leading to the east portal. Cramming more shanties for enslaved laborers in that confined space would not have been Claudius Crozet's preference, bearing in mind his reservations about allowing the races to mix. And, if Farrow and Hansbrough wanted shanties for housing the enslaved laborers, those structures would have been on state property. The detailed contract that the two men signed contained no regulation for shanty construction that appeared on other Blue Ridge Railroad agreements.[82]

BLANKET AND HAT

As the Farrow, Hansbrough and Ramsey men slaved at the Blue Ridge Tunnel in 1854, work continued on the temporary track. William Sclater, unsuccessful at finding slave labor for the hazardous tunnel, had no trouble convincing Albemarle County slaveholders that renting out slave labor for track bed preparation was a safer bet. He hired two foremen, one for each side of Rockfish Gap. George Harris was in charge of unmarried men on the west slope in Augusta County. On the east side, James H. Jarman controlled the married, enslaved men. They were delegated to him so they could be nearer their wives for allowed visits.[83]

Four of the slaveholders had ties with the University of Virginia—the nearby state institution that had used slave labor for construction, just as the state-financed Blue Ridge Railroad was doing now. One of the slaveholders was Socrates Maupin, a University of Virginia graduate who became a professor of chemistry and pharmacology in 1853. In 1854, the same year that the faculty elected him chairman—the equivalent of university president today—he leased the labor of a man named Dabney to the Blue Ridge Railroad. Maupin knew that railroad construction across the state was raising rates for hired slave labor. In the late 1840s, he had rented out, for $75 a year, one of the five people he enslaved. Now he could double that amount. The Blue Ridge Railroad Company returned Dabney with the customary clothing of a blanket and hat and paid Maupin $150 in January 1855.[84]

This is to Certify, That C. CROZET, CHIEF ENGINEER OF THE BLUE RIDGE RAIL-ROAD, in obedience to a Resolution adopted by the Board of Public Works of Virginia, on the 10th day of December 1853, has hired of *Dr. Socrates Maupin*

for one year from the *1st* day of *January* 1854 *one* negro man, named *Dabney*

to be employed upon the Work under the charge of the said Chief Engineer; in consideration whereof, the said Board of Public Works are to pay to the said *S. Maupin* his heirs or assigns, — *One hundred and fifty* dollars, payable *on the 1st day of January Eighteen hundred and fifty-five* and to furnish the said negro during the year with the customary Clothing.

WITNESS the signature of the said Chief Engineer this *9th* day of *January* 1854

C. Crozet

Ritchies & Dunnavant, Prs.—Richmond, Va.

Contract between Claudius Crozet and Socrates Maupin for the labor of Dabney. *Author's collection.*

Alfred Mosby was the father of John Singleton Mosby, who would become a commander in the Confederate army. John received a ten-year sentence for shooting a fellow University of Virginia student in 1852. The governor of Virginia pardoned him in late 1853, but a $500 fine (later rescinded) hung over the family's head. The elder Mosby hired out the labor of Ellis, Ben and Scipio to the Blue Ridge Railroad from July 1854 to January 1855. Perhaps the oddly timed, out-of-season lease helped him recover money he had spent on his son's legal fees. The state paid him $65 for the labor of each man.[85]

Charles Carter, a Charlottesville physician who treated University of Virginia students, cared for the young man John Mosby shot, and he signed a petition that led to Mosby's pardon. Carter held ten people in slavery in 1850. Two of them, Remus and Romulus Bracket, were twin brothers born around 1810. Carter assigned them to wait on his daughter, wife of university proctor Green Peyton. Then, as eager as other slaveholders to take advantage of rising rates for hired slaves, he leased the labor of Bob, George and the forty-four-year-old Bracket brothers to the railroad on January 1, 1854. Carter's income from their toil totaled $600.[86]

Aside from the thirty-one slaves listed under his and Christopher Valentine's names on the 1850 slave schedule, Thomas Jefferson Randolph personally enslaved twenty-one people. As far as we know, he hired none of them to William Sclater in 1854. But his tenure as a member of the Board of Visitors at the University of Virginia and serving six times in the Virginia House of Delegates placed him in a position of influence. In 1854, he tried using his influence for recovery of, as he put it, "not less than $1,000" for lost slave labor wages in 1852.[87]

Claudius Crozet had failed to keep his word when he guaranteed that the Randolph-Valentine hands would not be idle after the state-hired force helped finish sections seven and eight. "The work was completed some days before Christmas [1852]," Randolph recalled in a letter to the Board of Public Works, "and the employment was not given as promised whereby an additional cost was incurred for which I deem compensation just."[88]

Randolph and Valentine maintained a crew of fifty-one men in 1851. If that number held fast for 1852, and if the enslaved men exerted no railroad labor for twenty days before Christmas 1852, an estimated cost of $1 daily for their labor, food and clothing multiplies to a loss of $1,020. The amount is close to what Randolph claimed the state owed him.

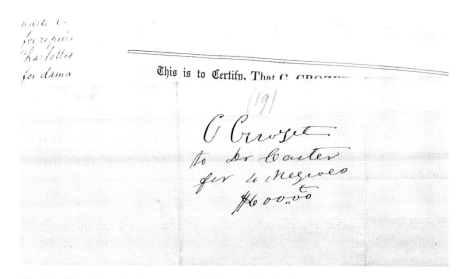

Claudius Crozet's receipt for payment of $600 to Charles Carter. *Author's collection.*

SCHEDULE 2.—Slave Inhabitants in _____ in the County of *Albemarle* State of *Virginia*, enumerated by me, on the *7th* day of *Aug't*, 1850. *John J Winn* Ass't Marshal

	NAMES OF SLAVE OWNERS	Number of Slaves	Age	Sex	Colour	Fugitive from the State	Number manumitted	Deaf & dumb, blind, insane, or idiotic
1	Thos J Randolph	10	23	M	M			
2			22	M	M			
3			23	M	M			
4			41	M	M			
5			20	M	M			
6			19	M	M			
7			17	F	B			
8			16	M	M			
9			16	M	M			
10			15	F	B			
11			18	M	M			
12			22	F	B			
13			10	F	M			
14			11	F	B			
15			20	M	M			
16			17	M	M			
17			11	M	M			
18			7	M	M			
19			5	F	M			
20			3	F	M			
21			1	F	B			
22	John Hall	1	2	F	B			
23	Richard Durrett	1	12	F	B			
24	William Dowell	3	12	F	B			
25			9	F	B			
26			7	F	B			
27	David S Martin	2	17	F	B			
28			13	F	B			
29	Henry Bruce	1	60	M	B			
30			25	F	B			
31			14	F	B			
32			8	M	B			
33			6	F	B			
34			5	F	B			
35			3	F	B			
36			7/12	F	B			
37	William S Moore	1	25	F	B			
38	John Roberts	4	60	M	B			
39			55	M	B			
40			40	F	B			
41			3	M	B			
42	William Blackwell	4	60	F	B			

	NAMES OF SLAVE OWNERS	Number of Slaves	Age	Sex	Colour	Fugitive from the State	Number manumitted	Deaf & dumb, blind, insane, or idiotic
1	Wm Blackwell continued		45	F	B			
2			17	M	B			
3			8	F	B			
4	Lewis Snow	3	43	F	B			
5			19	M	B			
6			5	F	B			
7	Early Marshal	5	40	M	B			
8			30	F	B			
9			25	M	B			
10			9	M	B			
11			1	M	B			
12	William Catterton	21	90	F	B			
13			35	M	B			
14			35	F	B			
15			35	F	B			
16			23	M	B			
17			17	M	B			
18			14	M	B			
19			15	F	B			
20			12	M	B			
21			11	F	B			
22			9	M	B			
23			9	M	B			
24			9	M	B			
25			9	M	B			
26			4	F	B			
27			4	F	B			
28			3	F	B			
29			2	F	B			
30			1	M	B			
31			70	F	B			
32			15	M	B			
33	Marshal D Elliott	6	22	M	B			
34			4	F	B			
35			25	F	B			
36			14	M	B			
37			6	F	B			
38			2	F	B			
39	Elizabeth Dunn	2	21	F	B			
40			19	M	B			
41	Leland Blackwell	11	40	M	B			
42			40	F	B			

Top left: Unnamed enslaved people listed under Thomas Jefferson Randolph's name on the federal slave schedule, Albemarle County, Virginia, 1850. *National Archives.*

Westbound Amtrak Cardinal heading toward what was section seven of the Blue Ridge Railroad construction. *Paul Collinge, 2019.*

Thomas Jefferson Randolph's enslavement of people and the profit he made from them present a conundrum. As a state delegate, he had proposed legislation in 1832 that called for the gradual abolition of slavery, albeit in a deeply cruel fashion. All children born after 1840 would have automatically become the property of the state, which would then compensate slaveholders for the monetary loss. When enslaved males reached the age of twenty-one and enslaved females the age of eighteen, the slaveholders would hire them out until they had earned enough money to pay for their transportation to the west coast of Africa. Threatened by the forfeiture of people they thought of as property, Randolph's fellow delegates defeated the resolution.[89]

It is clear that the usefulness of hired-out slave labor as proposed in his resolution stayed with Randolph from the 1830s through his railroad building years in the 1840s and 1850s. To be fair, he professed he was not seeking gain for himself. "I hereby transfer to Mr. Christopher Valentine all my interest in such claim," he wrote to the Board of Public Works, "and authorize him to apply for and receive the same." A clerk's notation of the back of his letter reveals the fate of the petition: "4 Sept 1854. The Board decline to pay the claim."[90]

POOR FELLOWS

Thanks to track bed preparation by William Sclater's enslaved crew and Irish hands who then laid the rails, the temporary track opened to passenger traffic on March 20, 1854. Hastily constructed over Rockfish Gap in just seven months, the line was frighteningly steep on both sides of the mountain. Locomotives and cars could barely negotiate the tight bend at the peak, which was seven hundred feet above the unfinished Blue Ridge Tunnel. The journey terrified travelers who had never gone faster than the speed of a horse.

Descent on the west side was especially perilous; four people died on the slope between March and May. The first was a white employee of the Virginia Central, which by now controlled this portion of the line. He jumped off a runaway passenger car and fell ahead of it on the tracks. The car cut off both legs. He lived only a few hours after his massive injury.[91]

Jerry, held in slavery by James Garland; Thomas, enslaved by Andrew Woods; and a man held by one Mr. Tilman were in an accident on the west slope of Rockfish Gap on April 6, 1854. All were part of William Sclater's Albemarle County hired-out crew and supervised by overseer George Harris. On the afternoon of Tuesday, April 4, Harris ordered Jerry, Thomas, the Tilman fellow and some of Robert P. Smith's forty state-hired enslaved men to load five flatcars. The cargo was soil for a Blue Ridge Railroad embankment at the bottom of the western slope. With the locomotive in front of the flatcars, the engine man made successful deliveries on Tuesday and Wednesday. The enslaved men, accompanied by Harris, rode with the cargo down the hill and unloaded.[92]

But on Thursday morning, while George Harris was eating breakfast, the engine man inexplicably reversed the sequence. Now the flatcars were ahead of the locomotive going down the west side of Rockfish Gap. Harris was not aboard when a cracked bolt pin that connected the first flatcar to the locomotive broke. Brakeless, the flatcars began rolling down the seventy-two-feet-to-the-mile grade. Their speed was moderate at first. In testimony given in front of the Board of Public Works in November, the engine man said he "hollered to hands to jump off."[93]

Claudius Crozet described the rest of the scene for the Board of Public Works: "Some of the negroes had jumped off; the others, poor fellows, feeling safe, were actually laughing at their adventure; and would certainly have been safe, but for the unaccountable circumstance of a flat having been left in the curve beyond the Waynesboro' depot, standing right in the main track."[94]

This is to Certify, That C. CROZET, CHIEF ENGINEER OF THE BLUE RIDGE RAIL-
ROAD, in obedience to a Resolution adopted by the Board of Public Works of Virginia, on
the 10th day of December 1853, has hired of *James Garland*

for one year from the *1st* day of *January* 1854 *one* negro man, named
Jerry

to be employed upon the Work under the charge of the said Chief Engineer; in considera-
tion whereof, the said Board of Public Works are to pay to the said *James Garland*
his
heirs or assigns, *One hundred and fifty*
dollars, payable *1st of January Eighteen hundred and fifty-five*
and to furnish the said negro during the year with the customary Clothing, *hat & blanket*

WITNESS the signature of the said Chief Engineer this *9th* day of *January*
185*4*

C. Crozet

Ritchies & Dunnavant, Prs.—Richmond, Va.

Contract between Claudius Crozet and James Garland for the labor of Jerry. *Author's collection.*

For Jerry, Thomas and the Tilman man, the whoosh of air on their
cheeks in the open flatcars must have felt akin to freedom—until a speed
of thirty-six-miles an hour paralyzed them with indecision. Unchecked,
the cars reached the bottom of the slope, crossed the South River Bridge
and passed the Waynesboro Depot. Then they collided with the stationary
car. William Sclater, who was not present at the accident, heard that the
Tilman man was "at first to lie very seriously injured, but he walked
home the other day has none of his limbs broken can't tell what is his
real injury."[95]

Jerry and Thomas were killed. William Sclater blamed the engine man
for running the locomotive behind the flatcars. George Harris, whose job
was to ride with and direct the enslaved men, claimed he had gone with
the hands on every train but this one. His presence was unnecessary, he
said in his defense, because it "was under the management of the engine
man and many firemen who came with it." Claudius Crozet testified that
descending the mountain with the locomotive leading the flatcars would

have been safer, but it was the "car on the other side of the bridge," he stated, "that produced the accident."[96]

This was a "hard case," Crozet privately admitted at his temporary quarters in Brooksville Inn. "There ought to be compensation in some way," he said, "[and] probably the legislature would pay." Crozet's observation was perceptive. The west side tracks were under Virginia Central Railroad control at the time of the calamity, yet the state carved out monies set aside for the Blue Ridge Railroad to reimburse the slaveholders:

> *Claims for compensation have been presented against the Board of P. Works by Garland and Wood of Albemarle for slaves hired by the claimants to the Board, & killed while in the employment of the latter on the Blue Ridge Railroad, and I understand my opinion to be desired by the Board on the question raised by these claims.*
>
> *On the evidence that I have seen including that which was given before the Board orally in my presence, and on consideration of the legal questions that present themselves to my mind or have been suggested by the Board, I am of opinion that the Board is liable for reasonable compensation and may apply to that use so much as necessary out of the money appropriated for the construction of the Road.*
>
> *Some papers having relation to the subject were said to be in possession of the Board, namely the contract between Col. Crozet and the President of the Central R. Road about the hauling that these slaves were engaged in when killed;—& possibly some others. These I have not seen but I am not able to perceive how they could vary the result.*
> *W.P. Bocock atty Gen*
> *Nov 1. 1854*
> *For the B. of P. Works*[97]

The board based its compensation on affidavits from three white men who were familiar with Jerry and Thomas. Of Jerry's value, Samuel White stated, "I have known the slave Jerry all his life. His character was remarkably good he was about twenty-one years of age, his personal appearance was very fine he being tall and strait [*sic*], his health was perfectly good. I think the negro worth at least twelve hundred and fifty dollars. Indeed had I owned him, I would not have taken that amount for him knowing him so well as I did."[98]

William P. Jarman, who enslaved cart boy James Williams, testified that he had known Jerry for eight years. "I believe Jerry's character to be very good," said Jarman, "his age was about twenty one, his personal appearance

This is to Certify, That **C. CROZET**, CHIEF ENGINEER OF THE BLUE R₁

Claudius Crozet's receipt for payment of forty-five dollars to James Garland for the labor of Jerry. *Author's collection.*

was very good, being tall strait [*sic*] and well formed—his health was very good never having known him to be sick. I think he was worth at least eleven hundred Dollars at the time of his death."[99]

As to Thomas, William Sclater had only known him since his hiring-out on January 1, 1854. "He was a good working hand about twenty years old about six feet high," Sclater said, "of good appearance excepting a small scar on his temple where he had been burned and as far as I know healthy." Sclater estimated that Thomas was worth twelve hundred dollars.[100]

None of the official documents associated with the accident expressed regret, mentioned grieving family members or identified places of burial. The words were as dry as the paper on which they were written. Only Crozet voiced emotion. It was an "unfortunate accident," he wrote to the board, and he was "happy to add that the third negro, whose life was at first despaired of, is now out of danger."[101]

The single shred of personal information we have about Jerry and Thomas is that they were always hired out together, making the simultaneous death of two friends a double tragedy.[102]

I HAD HIM BURIED

A third hired-out slave under William Sclater's control died at Rockfish Gap on May 25, 1854. Sclater blamed the deceased when he wrote to slaveholder John Maupin in White Hall, Virginia:

> *Dear Sir, I am sorry to inform you that your Negro man Sam was killed yesterday evening with a hand car. he was the brakeman in the cars and his car run behind all the rest, and instead of his starting where the other cars did he waited until the others were half way to where they were going. he then let his go let it run as fast as it could and by that means run it off the track and pitched him over and killed him on the spot he did not live ten minutes. I had several times cautioned them against letting their cars run too fast & so has Mr. Harris but as Mr Harris had a little business and went over to Waynesborough, he said he had not been gone half an hour before he was killed. I suppose he thought as Mr Harris was not there he would run as fast he ~~choose~~ pleased not thinking of the danger until it was too late. I am very sorry but it can't be helped now*
> *[To] Mr. John Maupin*
> *Yours Respectfully*
> *Wm. Sclater*
> *I had him buried in the graveyard at Waynesborough* [103]

Here is how Claudius Crozet described the accident:

> *On the west side of the mountain, another gang is employed in raising the long embankment, which has settled a good deal....This section of the work has been unfortunate: I have given you before an account of the accident by which two negroes lost their lives; and I have again to report the loss of another on the 25th Ult.—while going down, as usual, on a hand car, the wheel on which the brake acts and also the axle broke, and the car, after having continued some 30 ft on the track in that condition, suddenly jumped the rail and turned over, down the embankment, catching the poor fellow and killing him instantly: why he did not jump off in time, I have not understood.* [104]

John Maupin certainly would have known about the state's compensation for the deaths of Jerry and Thomas. He, too, wanted reimbursement for loss of so-called property. In February 1855, he

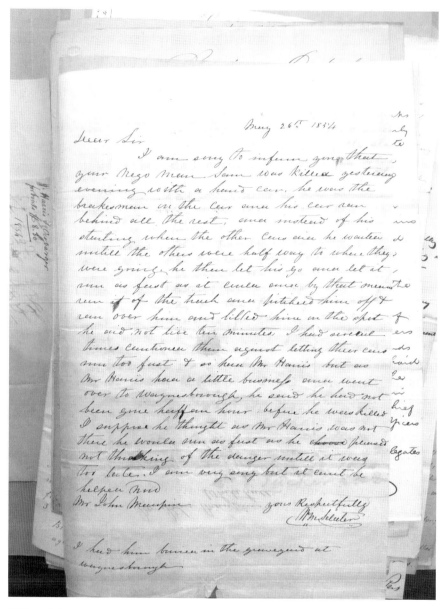

William Sclater's letter to John Maupin informing him of Sam's death. *Author's collection.*

engaged a law firm to prepare affidavits as evidence for the Board of Public Works. Under oath, George Harris explained that he had hired Sam, and the slaves were delivering soil in handcars to the embankment in Waynesboro. The accident occurred one half mile from town while Harris was voting in an election. "Both the axletree and wheel were broken," he said. "The wheel was mashed all to pieces."[105]

Estimating Sam's value, Harris gave his age at "about twenty years. His color was tolerably bright. He was undersize a little, he was about five feet four inches. He was a very likely boy—he was very healthy—I think he was worth about eleven hundred dollars."[106]

"He was about twenty," William Sclater testified. "I suppose you might call him a brown skin and about five feet four or five feet [inches] high. a very good appearance & healthy as far as I knew he was worth about one thousand dollars at that time."[107]

James H. Jarman, supervisor of Sclater's crew on the east side tracks, said that Sam's age was "twenty or twenty-one—he was a dark mulatto—He was five feet six inches tall—I suppose—he was very likely & as far as I know perfectly healthy—I have known him since he was twelve years old—he was worth a thousand or twelve hundred dollars—the way negroes were selling at that time."[108]

In the petition that followed, Maupin's lawyers pointed out that "this is the third negro killed by the cars running too rapidly down the mountain. The Board has already determined that the want of brakes on the car even when a white person was in charge constituted such neglect as to render them liable."[109]

And the petition maintained, "The overseer in charge of them left his gang without any white person to superintend it and went to an election. It appears moreover, that the car had been out of order and was just from the shop where it had undergone repairs on one of the fore wheels, and that one of the fore wheels was broken by the accident."[110]

The petition ended with the comment that the Board of Public Works was legally bound to compensate John Maupin. State attorney general W.P. Bocock thought otherwise. "From the written statements," he wrote on the back of the petition, "I do not advise the payment of this claim." Just below his words, a clerk noted, "Claim not allowed May 8, 1855."[111]

Tragically, William Sclater, who barely knew Sam, could choose when and where to bury him. If the young man had family members living on Maupin's farm, they would have cared for his remains and arranged the burial, perhaps in a cemetery for enslaved people on the property. The

Looking toward the original Blue Ridge Tunnel west portal. The gentle grade seen here steepens as it proceeds west down the mountain. *Wayne Nolde, 2019.*

location of the cemetery in Waynesboro where he was interred—without a headstone, no doubt—may never be determined. The best we can hope for Sam now is that some of his fellow laborers were present at the burial to speak a few words or sing a farewell spiritual by the grave.[112]

MYSTERIOUS DISEASE

Disastrous events on the Blue Ridge Railroad in 1854 continued through the summer. A vicious cholera epidemic struck Irish living on the east side of the Blue Ridge Tunnel during the last week of July. By month's end, twelve Irish were dead, with more deaths to come. Overseer William Ramsay drove the enslaved crew for seven days straight that week. This was doubtless an effort to make up for the loss of white labor in the passage.[113]

On Friday, July 28, the enslaved men had the dark tunnel mostly to themselves; of the 150 Irish on the east side, only 5 reported to work. As cholera spread on the east side, Ramsay finally removed the enslaved crew and kept them away for the first two weeks of August. In the meantime, the disease spread across the mountain and struck Irish in shanties on the west side of the tunnel. On August 10, one hundred west side Irish laborers and family members crowded aboard a train bound for Staunton, hoping they could escape a hideous death from massive diarrhea and dehydration. One newspaper called their exodus a "regular stampede."[114]

After returning to the east side of the Blue Ridge Tunnel on August 14, William Ramsay's crew labored for one six-day week. He gave them a day of rest on Sunday and then pushed them hard through nine days of labor in a row. Again, they were making up for the lack of Irish hands. Beyond August, Ramsay held the men to a tight schedule; only a few missed a full day of labor from September through year's end. Blacksmiths were in particular demand. Abraham, Thomas Barns and Robert Mickums often endured one and a half shifts—at least twelve straight hours—as they sharpened tools by the flickering orange glow of their forges. The long shifts guaranteed that their enslavers received the full contractual wages of $1.40 a day. If one of the smiths missed half a day of labor, he made it up with a one-and-a-half shift before the week ended.[115]

As the Christmas hiring-out season fast approached in early December, enslaved men at the tunnel would have looked forward to the traditional holiday break of two or three days. Though none could be sure where he would end up when the hiring-out cycle began again in the new year, more than a few must have hoped their time in the gloomy bore would soon be over.

Claudius Crozet had other plans. He told the Board of Public Works that the "gang of negroes" who had trimmed and ballasted the track beds were finished with the job and unnecessary for 1855. But the Blue Ridge Tunnel was a different situation. John Kelly and John Larguey—Irish contractors

Blasted approach to the east portal of the Blue Ridge Tunnel, 2016. *Author's collection.*

for the passage—advised Crozet, "It will be advantageous to hire as many negroes as practicable for the Tunnel."[116]

Natives of predominantly Catholic Ireland, Kelly and Larguey knew that most Irish Catholic laborers refused to work on feast days because the church designated them as holy days of obligation. Christmas was the Feast of the Nativity, January 1 was the Feast of the Circumcision and January 6 was the Feast of the Epiphany. The church required attendance at Mass on these and many other holy days throughout the year. The parish priest in Staunton had asked the Irish to build a wooden chapel at the top of Rockfish Gap for his occasional visits. But, spread thin across several parishes in the region, he was not always able to say Mass at the chapel. Mass or not, the Irish observed holy days by absenting themselves from work.

The men also missed work for wakes and funerals, especially during the "sickly year," as Claudius Crozet labeled the time of cholera. Slave labor in the coming year of 1855 would ease any labor interruption the Irish might cause, be it a strike, feast day or burial of a "mere child," as he put it. He reviewed the facts for the board:[117]

It was difficult last year to hire negroes for the Tunnel; but now the nature of the work is better understood and I think we can obtain a greater number. There is, however, some difficulty at present to fix the price of hire, while things are so unstable; and yet it is important to secure hands before christmas, in order that they may be on the work soon thereafter. Probably, if the Board will again hire negroes, the safest plan would be to do so upon some sliding scale regulated by the price of white labor; I believe some such bids will be submitted to you.[118]

Conditions along the Blue Ridge Railroad were ever changing, and December 1854 was no exception. December 23 was the last day for enslaved laborers at the Blue Ridge Tunnel. Sometime late that month, the Board of Public Works voted against slave labor in the tunnel for the following year. The high cost of compensation for the deaths of Jerry and Thomas must have made them wary, and George Farrow's 1854 contract required that the state compensate him even for a slave's injury. Board members may have wanted to avoid facing another year of potential added expense.[119]

"Bonds for the hire of negroes," page two, December 1854. *Author's collection.*

Claudius Crozet was calm about the board's decision, for he now had the Irish over a wages barrel. Spiritless after the cholera epidemic and defeated by the thought of competing against a possibly lower rate of slave labor pay, the Irish made no protest when Crozet dropped the salary for most of them back to the pre–1853 strike level of one dollar a day. He shared his pleasure with the board:[120]

Gentlemen,

I have the honor to report, that the recent facility of obtaining white hands, has enabled us to reduce the price of labour in both Tunnels to one dollar, which is as low a rate as the lowest price at which we were offered negroes. In consequence of this favorable change, and seeing that, at your last meeting, you inclined to the opinion not to employ negroes, I concluded that, under present circumstances, it was not advisable to mix again white and black labor in the tunnel.

Nor shall we want any longer a gang outside; the negroes, engaged during the past season in completing the 12 miles in use by the Central railroad Company, having finished this work: indeed, they had some time to spare, which I turned to advantage in causing them to fill up the time, by preparing the ballasting, and otherwise improving the unfinished sections; which are now ready for the track.[121]

5
1855–56

I REGRET THAT WE DID NOT HIRE NEGROES

Work was slower than ever on the Blue Ridge Railroad at the start of 1855. True, Greenwood Tunnel was finished, and Little Rock Tunnel was almost complete. The temporary track, opened by now for eight months, was an enormous success. But rotting timbers and falling rocks created unstable conditions for men boring through the Blue Ridge and Brooksville Tunnels. In February, three Irishmen were "dreadfully wounded and mangled," according to one newspaper report, when a faulty charge of gunpowder exploded in the Blue Ridge Tunnel. One of the men died two days later, probably in unspeakable pain. As happened almost every year on the Blue Ridge Railroad, the gruesome accident instigated an Irish strike. "I regret that we did not hire negroes at Christmas," Crozet admitted after the strike began in March. He reported conditions to the board:[122]

> *Gentlemen,*
> *The steady progress of the main Tunnel, which I thought I had every reason to expect, has been suddenly interrupted in a manner which I was far from anticipating at this time.—the Irish employed on the work have struck for higher wages.—Even in my last communication, I expressed my satisfaction that we had those men now under better control, and cannot conceive that they have ventured upon such a step when so many are*

seeking work—The only reasonable explanation, which is not altogether groundless, is that they have been tampered with; but I have not yet been able to arrive at proofs.[123]

IMPLEMENTS AND TOOLS AT THE BLUE RIDGE TUNNEL:

Hammers
Drills [augers]
Axes
Wagon and cart wheels
Shovels
Hinges
Padlocks
Hand and hack saws
Horseshoes
Tongs
Vises
Hack saws
Crow bars
Files
Rasps*

Claudius Crozet made no mention in his March letter of enslaved men he had rehired. Master blacksmiths Abraham and Robert Mickums showed up at the Blue Ridge Tunnel in January 1855, along with Wesley Carter, who now worked as a smith. Master smith Thomas Barns joined the others in February. The Blue Ridge Railroad certainly needed them all. With only two Irish blacksmiths for the east side of the bore in January, Crozet and his Irish contractors were in desperate want of skilled men to sharpen drills that dulled after a few hours of grinding against hard greenstone. The 150 men and boys working on the east side of the passage that month used a variety of tools and implements. All the devices eventually required a blacksmith's rapid repair, which meant a long trek through the smoky bore and outside to the smithy sheds.[124]

A visitor to the east side of the tunnel described such a scene: "We saw a dim speck of light approaching us. As it came nearer, we saw a huge indefinite form that was carrying it….It was nothing but a big Irishman with a lot of augers on his shoulder taking them out to get them sharpened. We went on a little farther and the smoke and stench became so intolerable that we turned and made for the spot of light we could see, where we came in."[125]

Crozet's manipulation of Irish wages in December 1854 lowered pay for blacksmiths in the tunnel from $1.40 to $1.30 a day in 1855. The rate applied to both black and white smiths. But to Crozet's chagrin, the weeklong Irish strike gave him no choice—he soon raised wages for the more skilled laborers. By July, the rate of pay for all smiths, black and white, was up to $1.42½ a day.[126]

* Blue Ridge Tunnel account book, 1851–57, BRP.

David Hansbrough—George Farrow's brother-in-law—claimed as his property all four of the enslaved blacksmiths who labored, on and off, at the Blue Ridge Tunnel in 1855 and 1856. The 1854 Farrow-Hansbrough contract with the state was specific, suggesting that both slaveholders were sticklers for a protective legal document. But no post-1854 contract for hiring out these blacksmiths has been found. Maybe Hansbrough allowed them to self-hire and keep some of the wages. Such an arrangement occasionally occurred in the antebellum South, depending on the whim of the enslaver.[127]

WADE IN BLOOD

James Williams turned thirteen years old midway through his time as a cart boy for Robert Smith in 1853. It is unknown if William Jarman rented Williams for railroad labor after that year, but the slaveholder continued enjoying income that the young man brought in. During Williams's adolescent years, Jarman rented his labor to an Albemarle County distillery. "I helped make a lot of whiskey," Williams later remembered, "and then I worked awhile for the same people at the Mudwall Tavern in Charlottesville."[128]

The Mudwall Tavern stood on land now occupied by the First Baptist Church on West Main Street. Built a few yards north of Virginia Central Railroad tracks, the first structure on the site was a temperance hotel for University of Virginia students. A wall made of ochre-tinted Albemarle County clay soil fronted the building, leading to its name. The hotel, which allowed no alcohol, failed and then opened as a saloon. Obviously, Jarman permitted Williams to travel to and from the Mudwall with no supervision, though how often is unknown. The young man could have journeyed most of the way by train, but that mode was expensive on a daily basis. It could also be risky for an enslaved man to be out and about by himself.[129]

In 1856, William Jarman owned a hotel less than two hundred yards from Mechum's River Depot, the eastern end of the Blue Ridge Railroad. He was the postmaster at Mechum's and would have had a so-called body servant. The following newspaper article might have concerned James Williams or another man enslaved by Jarman:

> On Sunday last as the cars were ascending the mountain above Mecham
> [sic] river, the engineer discovered a negro man belonging to Mr. Jarman

Lower center: Eastbound locomotive entering Charlottesville, Virginia, 1856. *Top center*: Monticello. *Bottom*: University of Virginia. *Engraving by Casimir Bohn, Library of Congress.*

on the track, and being desirous of catching him, he reversed the steam, and without blowing the whistle cautiously took the train to the immediate vicinity of the negro, without awaking him; then jumping down and seizing a stout stick, gave the fellow a severe chastising, laying the blows on well; the negro exclaiming, "for God's sake, master, let me go, for see my nag has got loose and is running off.[130]

Rather than shuttling to and from Charlottesville, it is more likely that James Williams resided at the Mudwall Tavern for the length of his hired-out year. It was near the Mudwall, Williams recalled, that he heard and saw Abraham Lincoln give a speech from a platform. When the tavern closed for the occasion, Williams and other enslaved males hired out to the tavern owner stole away and heard the talk from the edge of a crowd. Lincoln never spoke in Charlottesville, but the content of the unknown speaker's address was remarkably similar to Thomas Jefferson Randolph's 1832 resolution for the gradual abolition of slavery: All slaves twenty-one years of age or over should be freed immediately. Those younger should have been freed when they came of age.[131]

What happened next offers a keen glimpse of James Williams's thoughts about enslavement. When he returned to the tavern, he overheard fiery remarks from a prosperous slaveholder who had witnessed the speech. "Before I see my son have to saddle and bridle his own horse," the man declared, "and my daughter get up before daybreak and get our breakfast, I'll wade in blood up to my saddle skirts."[132]

James Williams never forgot those words. As will be seen, he would have good reason to recollect them after the Civil War began in 1861.

CRUEL AND BRUTAL ACTS

By late 1856, the temporary track was more than two years old and deteriorating. Charles Ellet, chief engineer for the Virginia Central, hired the labor of twelve enslaved men to maintain it. Each of them brought in $150 for their respective slaveholders that year. Ellet may have tasked the crew with fixing a slide at Robertson Hollow and what Claudius Crozet termed the "immense cuts preceding it."[133]

The long-awaited boring-through of the Blue Ridge Tunnel was in sight by November 1856. "As regards the most important work of the line the Rockfish tunnel," Claudius Crozet told the board, "there remains only, at this date 87 feet of the heading to perforate. In all probability, it will be through a few days before the 1st of January."[134]

That same November, a Blue Ridge Railroad vendor in Augusta County wrote his will. A widower, sixty-seven-year-old Sampson Pelter was a wealthy farmer and wagoner. He owned thirty-one horses and four farms worth about $29,000—almost $1 million in 2019—on the west side of Rockfish Gap. He also held in slavery eleven people who produced lucrative crops of potatoes, wheat and corn and hundreds of pounds of butter. Hannah, his housekeeper, was one of the enslaved women. While enslaved field hands farmed his four hundred acres, she maintained his residence by washing, cooking, cleaning and other domestic labor.[135]

Hannah's forced work may have involved much more than chores. Pelter's will stated that his three grown sons would inherit land. They would also have the "use and benefit" of the people he enslaved "during their natural life," with the exception of three boys: John, Junius and Abraham. These three children would be freed when they came of age. Further, Pelter bequeathed 158 acres to them. The evidence strongly suggests that he fathered them by

Hannah Harden, post–Civil War, no date. A handwritten notation at the bottom states, "Housekeeper of Sampson Pelter pre–Civil War." *Waynesboro, Virginia Public Library.*

the sexual coercion—in other words, rape—of his housekeeper, Hannah. (The will made no provision for her manumission.)[136]

Hannah's life in Pelter's spacious brick mansion must have been horrific at times. According to testimony in court papers filed on behalf of his wife, who died in 1851, Pelter subjected his spouse to "cruel and brutal" acts in the 1840s. These included an attempted poisoning, beatings and a five-month period in which he repeatedly raped his wife's niece—a minor—who was living in their house at the time. When a justice of the peace asked the niece if the occurrence was "frequent and habitual," she answered, "very frequent."[137]

While Hannah peeled potatoes and churned butter, Pelter conducted shady deals involving the Blue Ridge Railroad. For example, Pelter thought he could pocket a chunk of the state money that funded the road. His first venture was a devious real estate swap with Samuel B. Brown. It involved a house next to the Blue Ridge Tunnel west portal. Crozet described Pelter's manipulation in a letter to a friend:

> You know that Pelter's house near the western entrance of the tunnel is somewhat in our way and Mr. Kinney had engaged to buy it for the Company.—Now it happens that this property bought 18 months ago for $1,800 by Sampson Pelter, has been sold lately for $4,500!—Some say it is no real sale! however this may be, I have received the other enclosed rather singular letter about it—From which it would appear as if the present owner had bought the property just for the sake of the injury he is to receive.[138]

Crozet enclosed with his letter a missive from Samuel B. Brown that claimed the following:

> I shall be damaged seriously, for I find it very difficult to rent it in consequence of the nearness of the dwelling. To the mouth of the tunnel not only the building, but the lives of the tenants are greatly endangered by the blasting that may be necessary in prosecution [of the] work—this you see operates to my injury—and may entirely prevent my renting it. My object in addressing you, is to state to you, some of the many injuries that I will sustain, and to request you to inform me, what mode will be resorted to in assisting the damages and at what time it will take place, whether it will be settled before, or after the commencement of the work—please answer me as early as may suit your convenience.
> Yrs, Saml. B. Brown.[139]

A third player in this charade was Pelter's brother, James, who happened to be renting the house. His moving out would serve as proof of injuries. Whatever damages were awarded, and how the men divided them, is uncertain, but Pelter ended up owning the land again by 1856. He called it the "mountain farm" and the "Rockfish Gap stand" in his will.[140]

Pelter made a second land grab attempt to cash in on the railroad construction in 1855. It failed when Crozet, by then wise to his tricks, suggested that the Board of Public Works simply condemn the property. Despite Pelter's dishonesty and utter lack of moral character, the board agreed that Pelter and his extended family would supply some of their many horses for the Blue Ridge Tunnel. The Pelters also sold the Blue Ridge Railroad Company hammer handles and cords of wood. Hauling heavy items such as nails, iron and steel by wagon to the passage was another source of income for the family, courtesy of state funds.[141]

Claudius Crozet's prediction that laborers would bore through the Blue Ridge Tunnel by the end of 1856 was surprisingly correct. On December 29, Crozet, one contractor and a few assistant engineers stood by on the east side as two Irishmen on the west noisily pounded a drill through the greenstone. Finally, a two-inch hole appeared, and lantern light shone through. After six long years, the men had penetrated the mountain.[142]

The chief engineer and his companions toasted with whiskey, while the Irish dropped their tools and celebrated for the rest of the day. In the following weeks, numerous newspapers throughout the country announced the boring-through. None of the articles mentioned the enslaved group that had toiled in the passage or the people enslaved by Pelter whose labor supported his business with the Blue Ridge Tunnel. But all of them, one way or another, made the momentous event possible.

6
1857–58

FOR THE BOARD OF NEGROES

Claudius Crozet grappled with brick problems throughout the construction decade. "I fear," he wrote early on, "that brick cannot be made in this neighborhood sufficiently sound to withstand the presence of so heavy a super incumbent weight."[143]

The chief engineer was referring to brick culverts, which would create a danger if even one collapsed under the weight of a train. Still, a train wreck in the open air might be less disastrous than a falling tunnel ceiling that would bury passengers alive. The temporary solution during tunnel construction was the erection of timber frames. These braces supported unstable portions of the ceiling while Irish drillers and blasters advanced through the bores. The permanent solution for train travel was arching the Blue Ridge Railroad tunnels with quality bricks. Crozet's brick specification was typically rigorous: "Wherever brick may be used, it shall be well burnt and sound, and none but whole bricks shall be used, except where allowed in writing by the engineer. The joints are to be close, none to exceed one fourth of an inch at the exterior, in arches; and in all cases to be flushed up with mortar and neatly pointed. Only the neat measurement of the brickwork is to be allowed at the rate, whatever may be the size of the brick, of 19 (nineteen) bricks to one [square] foot."[144]

Claudius Crozet specified concentric arches of half bricks for brick culverts, such as this one on section three. *Allen Hale, 2016.*

A mixed-race crew in a North Carolina brickyard, 1896. *Right*: Horse-powered pug mill kneading clay. *Jim Graves, International Brick Collectors Association.*

For the fully arched Greenwood Tunnel—the first completed passage on the railroad—Crozet first relied on Robert F. Harris of Charlottesville. Harris gathered a crew of five white men, seven white boys between the ages of twelve and sixteen and nine enslaved men who set up a new brickyard in Waynesboro. Harris likely chose the location for its access to water and a supply of appropriate clay just below the surface of the ground.[145]

Brick making in the 1850s was a months-long process with tedious repetition. All, or almost all, of it was done by hand. The Harris laborers first shoveled clay from the ground in autumn. Exposed to the elements, the material cured as it repeatedly froze and thawed over the winter. Harris's crew may have built a horse-drawn pug mill for the next labor-intensive step, which took place in spring: adding water and working the softened clay until it was the right consistency for a mold. In the absence of a pug mill, the crew members would have kneaded the clay with their hands and feet.[146]

The next step called for a three-person relay team. An unskilled laborer, perhaps a boy, carried a lump of clay to a table, where a skilled brick molder rolled it in sand to keep it from sticking. The brick molder then pressed the clay in a sanded mold—somewhat like a floured bread loaf pan—that held one to six brick-shaped forms. Using a flat stick soaked in water, he scraped excess clay from the top of the mold. A third laborer carried the mold to a separate area and removed the shaped clay for an initial two days of drying.

Then the crew piled the bricks-to-be—one by laborious one—in alternating stacks that allowed the passage of air. The newly born bricks dried for two more weeks under a layer of straw or a roofed shed.[147]

The last step was firing. Harris's crew built at least two kilns from raw bricks and hauled 230 cords of wood for fuel. The men tended the ovens day and night, adjusting the fire so the bricks would dry sufficiently yet not heat to the cracking point. They made about 6,500 bricks a day, working six days a week. Crozet rejected 70,900 of the bricks as too green because they still held enough moisture to create a crumbling arch in freeze-thaw conditions. He estimated the number of usable bricks for the Greenwood Tunnel at 97,000.[148]

Robert Harris charged the state $42.00 for the board of the white men, $37.33 for the board of the boys and $45.00 for the "board of negroes," as listed in his account papers. If we use the rate of $0.70 a week that the state paid Hugh Gallaher for boarding enslaved men, the enslaved Harris crew labored for seven and a half weeks during the active brickmaking operation. Eventually, they produced 150,000 usable bricks for the Greenwood Tunnel. Added to these were batches made by Joseph Dettor of western Albemarle County and John W. Walker of Louisa County. The two slaveholders held an approximate total of nine men and boys of the right age to labor in their brickyards. Walker likely supplemented his enslaved force with one white brickmason, five white laborers and one free man of color—all were boarders at his Louisa residence.[149]

A perilous place in the Brooksville Tunnel ceiling called for an arch three feet thick constructed with 1.8 million bricks. Crozet informed the board that it "must be made strong enough, not only to resist great pressure, but also the fall of rocks from a considerable height." He considered nine brickmaking businesses while carefully assessing the location of their yards. This was crucial, as Brooksville Tunnel cut through a steep ridge bordered by deep hollows. The time and labor required to haul bricks up an almost vertical slope to the passage would be expensive.[150]

When Robert Richardson from Fluvanna County discovered a field of suitable clay very near the tunnel, Crozet settled on him. Richardson enslaved only one man, but census records show that he also depended on hired slave labor that could set up a new yard and produce bricks. The Brooksville Tunnel was finished by October 1856. Crozet declared that the bricks were of "excellent quality, capable of bearing, without crushing, from 900 to 2,400 pounds to the square inch."[151]

Right: Layers of loose bricks and other disintegrated material were removed during restoration of the Blue Ridge Tunnel. *Wayne Nolde, 2019.*

Below: Mortared bricks from the original Brooksville Tunnel after it was blown up for construction of Interstate 64. *Paul Collinge, 2016.*

FATAL CONSEQUENCES

The Little Rock Tunnel could stand on its own, leaving one passage left for arching: the all-important Blue Ridge Tunnel. A span of 200 feet on the west side was already arched in April 1857 when Claudius Crozet provided the board with an "exact account of the condition and requirements" for more west side brick work. Rocks on the ceiling of one 140-foot stretch were loose, but he assured the board, "There is no immediate danger in that section: not a single stone has ever fallen from the roof for 4 years, notwithstanding the powerful concussions from our heavy blasts in that confined space."[152]

Out of caution, Crozet thought another 735 feet on the west side might need a thin arch, but this could wait until the tunnel opened for trains. He reasoned, "It would be impossible to carry on simultaneously the operations of arching, together with the removal of the remaining block and the

Center background: The sixteen-foot-wide brick arch inside the Blue Ridge Tunnel east portal may have been a demonstration template. *Bob Dombrowe, 2018.*

Crumbling bricks removed during the Blue Ridge Tunnel restoration in 2019 revealed 1850s blasted rock. *Paul Collinge, 2019.*

leveling off of the floor; the two last employing already three cars constantly in motion on the track which impede each other materially and would be in the way of hauling bricks mortar and cement: But there will be no difficulty in arching while the trains shall be running through; it can be done easily after their passage and in the night, without either inconvenience or danger to anyone."[153]

One month later, Crozet changed his mind about the ceiling's stability:[154] "As regards the arching, a recent re-examination has confirmed my opinion of the necessity of that measure for 140 feet, and shaken my confidence in the ultimate safety of the remaining distance on the west side: I had examined the roof some six months ago and found that distance of 735 feet sound; but the late trial of the roof discloses the fact that time has a much more rapid and destructive effect on this rock than I had been led to suppose from its excessive hardness."[155]

Though the number of bricks on hand for a total of 875 feet of arching was insufficient, Virginia's general assembly chopped the Blue Ridge Railroad budget, leaving no money for more bricks. Crozet appealed to the president of the Virginia Central, hoping he would "assist us in this dilemma," as he told the board, but he was refused. Finally, the state allocated enough money to pay contractor John Kelly for brick acquisition. He chose John W. Walker, previously hired for the Greenwood Tunnel.

Crozet described Walker as a "very reliable and skilful [*sic*] brick maker." These were sorely needed qualities, as the production schedule would be fierce.[156] Walker's contract called for delivery of 100,000 bricks before June 20, 1857, and 600,000 before mid-October, when autumn tempering of the clay began. Come mid-April of the following year, his mixed-race force was to make 650,000 more bricks. The entire process would eat up valuable time. Crozet warned the board that waiting for the bricks and then installing the arch would consume nine months beyond April 1858—and this for a tunnel he had predicted would be finished in 1853.[157]

Safety was always Claudius Crozet's priority, but the public had long been impatient. By June and July of 1857, he was under siege when local citizens signed two petitions that questioned the necessity for more arching in the Blue Ridge Tunnel. Unaware of his conviction that nighttime work was safe, they maintained that arching, if needed, would endanger passengers. "The Travelling community feel great uneasiness," wrote the Augusta County petitioners, "in passing through a long tunnel under the most favorable circumstances; The fatal consequences of arresting a passenger train in the Rockfish Tunnel need not be depicted to you." The petitioners insisted that the board turn over completion of the passage to the Virginia Central Railroad. In July, directors of the Virginia Central passed resolutions that duplicated the citizen petitions.[158]

Slow state funding and a brick shortage, a stable ceiling one month but not the next, an uncooperative partner-railroad plus a restive yet fearful public—Crozet felt cornered by the fall of 1857. Still, over the next few months, he managed to solve the brick crisis by shortening the west side arch to 483 feet, pronouncing the remaining distance safe enough. He also found an escape from eight years of worry and obstacles at the Blue Ridge Railroad. In September 1857, the Virginia Central took charge, and by December, Crozet was a supervisory engineer for an aqueduct construction project in Washington, D.C.[159]

The crisis of public confidence was resolved when the permanent Blue Ridge Railroad and its four tunnels opened on April 13, 1858. The road was an astounding success. Between April and October, more than forty thousand passengers traveled through the Blue Ridge Tunnel for $0.50 each. Almost twenty-four thousand barrels of flour moved through for $0.10 each.

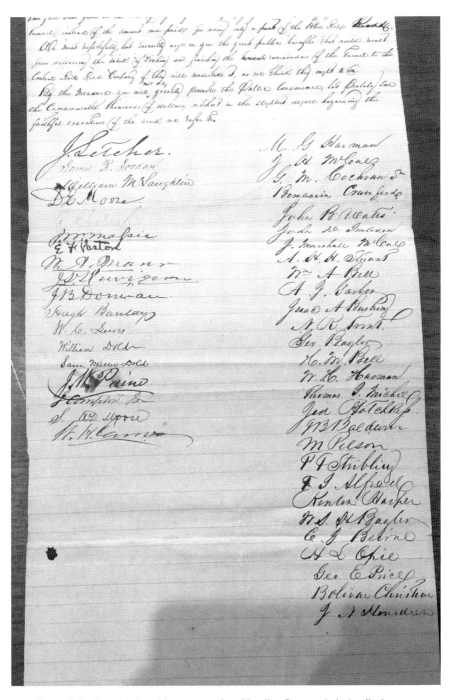

Page three of the June 1857 petition concerning Claudius Crozet. *Author's collection.*

East portal of the Blue Ridge Tunnel. *Jim Kauffman, 2015.*

The company earned 10 percent on all freight charges, bringing total profit for the six-month period to $38,538.00. Almost $27,000.00 of it went to the Virginia Central's bank account. The company sent the remainder to Virginia's treasury as partial payment for assuming the railroad.[160]

Scores of enslaved brickmakers made the historic opening of the Blue Ridge Railroad possible. The human equivalent of steam shovels and conveyor belts, they helped produce well over *three million* bricks. Though none could ride on the road without a handwritten pass from a slaveholder, their labor ensured the safe travel of train employees and passengers for the next eighty-eight years.[161]

1859–65

BALL OF FIRE

Use of slave labor on the Blue Ridge Railroad, by now the Virginia Central, diminished but did not disappear after the route opened. John S. Cocke, owner of the Long House Inn in western Albemarle County, hired out six men to the Virginia Central Railroad for the 1860–61 season. He could easily spare them. The number of people he enslaved increased from thirty in 1850 to forty-five in 1860.[162]

The men Cocke hired out probably performed usual maintenance tasks such as shoring up embankments and reapplying ballast. And in those pre-creosote days, railroad ties—especially in the damp Blue Ridge Tunnel—lasted only five years or less. The beginning signs of rot and need for future replacement would have been apparent. Six laborers were inadequate for almost seventeen miles of ties, rails, culverts and embankments. We can be sure the Virginia Central Railroad hired more slave labor to keep the road in working order.[163]

Now a grown man of twenty, James Williams's Blue Ridge Railroad days were long over. Still held in slavery, he was probably an in-house laborer for William Jarman. On occasional Sundays, he was a preacher, holding services with a chair back as his lectern. Enslaved people from nearby plantations whose owners gave permission for preaching took turns hosting the prayer meetings at their quarters. "Main thing we did," Williams recalled, "was exhort the slaves to be good and promise them they'd get an extra cup of coffee and a cake on Christmas morning if they were."[164]

Perhaps James Williams met the woman who would be his first wife at Sunday morning worship. They wed with no ceremony sometime before the Civil War began. As required by law, William Jarman gave permission by writing up a formal paper stating James Williams's age, name and other pertinent facts about him. Jarman exchanged this paper with the bride's owner, James Woods of Woods Mill on the Rockfish River in Nelson County. Woods gave Jarman her paper in return. The couple probably had an abroad marriage with occasional visits allowed.

William Jarman eventually moved his household from western Albemarle County to Wood's Mill. At this point, James Williams and his wife were likely within walking distance of each other, so more frequent conjugal visits would have occurred. The couple's subsequent two children became James Woods's property.[165]

In 1861, thirteen southern states seceded from the Union, and the fractured country began its wretched Civil War. James Williams's duties as a husband and father meant little to William Jarman, who faced the loss of twelve enslaved people if Union forces defeated the South. Jarman delivered him and his other enslaved men to the Richmond area, where they joined many hundreds more who were building Confederate breastworks. The grueling labor was made doubly hard by its foul purpose. As one formerly enslaved man later described it, "So the poor slaves were seized in every section, dragged brutally to different places, and forced under the scourge [whip] to build fortifications, not only against those in whose hands was held the proclamation of their emancipation, but to defeat if possible the men who sought to save the Union."[166]

Hauling earth for breast-high fortifications would have been a painful reminder to James Williams of his time as a cart boy on the Blue Ridge Railroad. When Williams resisted the breastwork labor, Jarman sent him to the Shenandoah Valley. Williams, along with other enslaved teamsters, drove horses back and forth between the Blue Ridge and Alleghany Mountains, hauling animal feed and transporting artillery horses for the Confederate army. He recalled that he drove a forage wagon for "quite some time."[167]

As far as we know, James Williams never tried to escape from slavery. It might seem that he had ample opportunity for flight while on the Blue Ridge Railroad and at the Mudwall Tavern. Some enslaved adolescents grabbed the opportunity when they could, though running away was exceedingly risky. The Emancipation Proclamation freed enslaved people

Woods Mill on the Rockfish River, Nelson County, Virginia, 2018. *Author's collection.*

in Confederate states on January 1, 1863, and Williams's labor on the Richmond breastworks during the war, plus his travels as a teamster, put him even farther away from the watchful eyes of William Jarman. But the number of white people—overseers, contractors and military personnel—who directed his life increased. Despite the proclamation, a successful getaway was nearly impossible.[168]

The slaveholder Williams overheard at the Mudwall Tavern turned out to have a surprising shortage of rebel yell spirit. It appears that the wealthy man's son who was incapable of bridling his own horse was also too weak for soldiering. "This particular gentleman," Williams remembered, "promised $500, five acres of land and a mule" to a poor mountain man if he would take his son's place.[169]

"He didn't say when he'd get all that," Williams recalled, "and a few days after the mountaineer agreed and went to war he was killed. Then the slaveholder refused to give the money, the land or the mule to the widow. In fact he put her out of her home altogether. Guess he wasn't as anxious to wade in blood as he said he was. But God punished him. Every night

Left and center: Black laborers pose with levers used to remove rails on a confiscated Confederate line in northern Virginia, circa 1862–63. *Library of Congress.*

after he'd put that poor widow out of house and home, a ball of fire rolled down the hill into the man's home until finally he was driven crazy and killed himself."[170]

James Williams said he never saw the ball of fire but heard about it from a guard hired to shoot it. The story has the flavor of folklore. We can almost hear Williams repeating it for other enslaved people. The tale's justice-served ending would have satisfied him and his listeners, all still shackled by chattel slavery.[171]

RUN OFF TO THE ENEMY

The need for hired slave labor in Virginia greatly increased during the Civil War, especially for the Virginia Central Railroad. Edmund Fontaine, president of the company, had predicted earlier that the line's great strength would be its route through slaveholding states: "Among the many sources of profit to which we can look, not the least is the fact that its location will secure to us the largest share of the immense travel from those states because it will be free from the annoyances which occur on lines running through the 'free soil' territory....Ours will be an important link in a chain of railroads reaching from the Atlantic to the Pacific not passing over a foot of abolition territory."[172]

But 1850s proslavery sentiment was of little help to Fontaine and the railroad in 1862. Confederate troops and supplies moved along every foot of the line, turning every mile into a potential battlefield. With Union forces ripping up railroad ties for firewood and destroying bridges along the route, Virginia Central tracks needed constant repair. Fontaine summarized the circumstances in his annual report: "The frequent raids made by the enemy on the road and its close proximity to the country[side] actually occupied by them, has produced some hesitation with the owners of slaves in hiring them to the company; and large numbers from the section of country supplying us with hands have either run off to the enemy or been carried off by them.[173]

Federal troops confiscated thirty enslaved men while restoring the line in 1862. Such events alarmed Virginia slaveholders. They became as cautious about hiring out slaves for railroad repair as they had been about letting them near explosions in the Blue Ridge Tunnel. In a broadside titled "To the Farmers Residing in the Vicinity of the Virginia Central Railroad,"

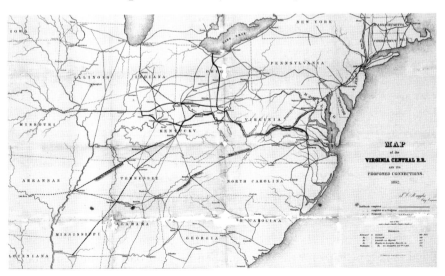

Map of the Virginia Central Railroad and its proposed connections, 1852. *Library of Congress.*

Fontaine made the following plea:

> *The imperative necessities of the war have deprived the Company of the usual supply of wood for the locomotives and cross-ties for repairing the Road, which heretofore have been furnished by contractors. Having now, to a great extent, to do what formerly was done by contractors, there is a demand for labor which the Company cannot supply without your assistance….In the existing state of things you alone can furnish the aid required. The labor we need to put this Road in safe working order cannot be obtained from any other resources than that which I think it is your interest to spare from your forces. Of* [white] *surplus labor, seeking hire, there is none….I will give* FORTY DOLLARS *per month for twenty-six working days for good laborers and find provisions….The fact stares you in the face that the Company needs a large number of hands. You all have them, and they are to be employed not for the benefit of the Stockholders as a corporation so much as for your own interests, being citizens occupying a section of country which cannot be defended unless the Road is put in good Order. E. Fontaine, President.* Office Va. Central Railroad
> *September 2, 1863*

Fontaine's postscript to his September announcement called for one hundred enslaved men, preferably equipped with axes. Of course, the high monthly rate of $40 he offered was inflated Confederate money. Three Confederate dollars bought one gold dollar at the time, and slaveholders knew it. Apparently, they ignored Fontaine's entreaty. In October, Virginia governor John Letcher approved the impressment of enslaved men for labor on the Virginia Central line, but more were needed. The company purchased thirty-five men for $83,484 in Confederate money and later bought still more.[174]

All came to naught when Confederate general Robert E. Lee surrendered to Union general Ulysses S. Grant in April 1865. James Williams was at William Jarman's estate on the Rockfish River when "Marse Billy" announced the news. During his twenty-five years of enslavement, Williams may or may not have endured whippings from Thomas, the older Jarman. "He never whipped any of us," Williams said, "unless we lied to him. He'd stand most anything but lying."[175]

But the younger Jarman certainly flogged Williams. While standing on the walkway that led to his big house, and with hands gripping white posts that lined the path, William Jarman announced to James Williams, "You're free. I don't own you anymore. I can't whip you anymore."[176]

Chesterfield Bridge over the North Anna River. Union troops destroyed it on May 25, 1864. *Timothy O'Sullivan, photographer, Library of Congress.*

Food deprivation was widespread across the South during and after the war. Some of the freed people on William Jarman's estate stayed on and harvested corn they had planted as field hands. We can hope that Jarman paid them or bartered a portion of the crop in exchange for picking it. But now that James Williams was free from whippings and forced labor, he could enlarge his world as he wished. Rather than pick corn, he moved west to neighboring Augusta County.[177]

8

1866–95

ALIKE AS TWO PEAS

A few precious facts are available about freedmen who labored on Blue
Ridge Railroad tracks. Twin brothers Remus and Romulus Bracket,
formerly enslaved by Charles Carter, remained in Charlottesville. For
decades after emancipation, Remus Bracket worked on a railroad.
This was either the Virginia Central (later the Chesapeake and Ohio)
or the Orange and Alexandria (now the Southern) that passed through
the city.[178]

Several scenarios are possible for Romulus Bracket's employment.
In 1870, he was living next to Robert F. Harris, the contractor who
supplied some of the bricks for the Greenwood Tunnel back in 1852.
Harris owned a foundry and residence in Charlottesville. Both stood on
West Main Street between Fourth and Fifth Streets Southwest. Identified
as a laborer in 1870, Bracket may have tended the cupola furnace at
the foundry, which produced agricultural implements. By 1880, he was
living in the Harris residence at the same West Main Street location
and identified on the census as an engineer. In the usage of the day, the
term could mean someone in charge of a fire or steam engine. Romulus
Bracket might have operated a steam engine in the foundry's woodshop
or manned a steam engine for the railroad, as tracks ran directly behind
the Harris foundry.[179]

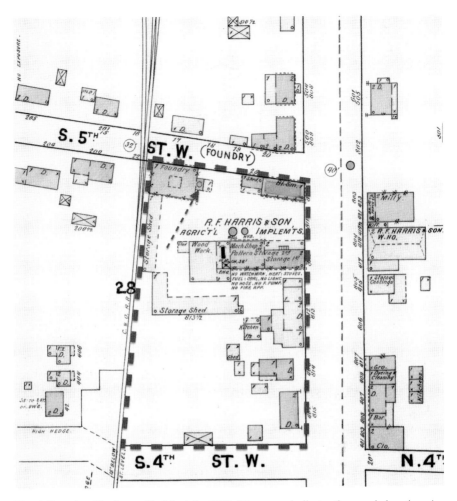

Harris Foundry, Charlottesville, Virginia, 1907. The arrow indicates the cupola location. A dumpster now occupies the space. *University of Virginia.*

Or Bracket could have been an engineer on the Charlottesville-University Street Railroad, a streetcar line. Robert F. Harris was an early investor in the company. In 1887, a long twenty years after incorporation, the line that ran from downtown Charlottesville to the university, along what is now Main Street, finally opened. It was an immediate success. If still alive (his date of death is unknown), the aging Romulus Bracket may have driven a team of mules—the engine—that pulled the car.[180]

Whatever the case, it is gratifying to know that the Bracket men finally received wages for their jobs. Remus Bracket died in 1899. His wife, Mary

Ann, died in 1923 and was buried at the Daughters of Zion Cemetery in Charlottesville. Both brothers may rest there in unmarked graves. Remus Bracket's obituary reads:

> OLD COLORED CITIZEN DEAD.
> *Remus Brackett, one of the oldest citizens of the city, died at his residence on Fourth street, east, at 8 o'clock this morning. He was 89 years of age. He had been ill for some time, but died from a simple failure of his faculties.*
> *Remus was a chattel in ante bellum [sic] times, of the late Dr. Charles Carter, and he and his twin brother, Romulus, were assigned to Dr. Carter's daughter, now Mrs. Green Peyton of the University. The two brothers were as much alike as two peas. Small in stature, with full beards and slow motions, they were ever prominent figures on the streets. Romulus died some years ago. They were both men of good characters and were respected by everyone. Remus will be buried tomorrow afternoon from the First Colored Baptist church.*[181]

Little is known about the men whose labor George Farrow leased to the Blue Ridge Tunnel. Possibly hoping for future recompense, he or a family member made a list of the fifty-four people he held in slavery at the surrender of Robert E. Lee. The list helps determine that most of the freed Farrow and nearby freed Hansbrough people were members of roughly six family groups, including those with the surnames of Hailstock and Spears.[182]

Reuben Hailstock, a floorer in the tunnel, lived with his family very near Farrow's Brooksville plantation after the war ended. William Spears inched west. In 1870, he and his daughter lived at Rockfish Gap in Nelson County. By 1880, they were in Augusta County, where he worked as a brickmason. In May 1865, blacksmith Thomas Barns and three other freed people agreed to provide services for their former enslaver, David Hansbrough. They completed the work but had to sue him for the wages in November. The court awarded Barns twenty-four dollars, minus two dollars for court costs. In 1880, he was living in the vicinity of the Mechum's River Bridge and was still a blacksmith.[183]

Samuel Carter, a floorer in the Blue Ridge Tunnel, did not live to see freedom. In 1863, the Confederacy forced him and other slaves to build breastworks throughout the South. His enslaved son, Willis, was eleven years old when George Farrow sent Samuel Carter away. Thirty years later, Willis Carter remembered that his father "was taken below Richmond Virginia to help fortify it where soon afterward, he had an attack of pneumonia which proved fatal."[184]

The historic Daughters of Zion Cemetery, Charlottesville, Virginia, 2019. Archaeologists have discovered evidence of at least three hundred unmarked graves. *Author's collection.*

Willis Carter grew up to be a nineteenth-century Renaissance man. With the help of the Goodloe family, who were Union supporters, he learned reading, writing and mathematics as a child. He later gave himself a classical education by "private study," as he called it. An impressive variety of jobs followed. He was a screw turner at the Goodloe mill, a firefighter, a flagman for the railroad, a hotel waiter, a porcelain factory worker, an amateur actor, a seminarian, a teacher, a school principal, a newspaper editor and a spokesperson for African American civil rights. Willis Carter obviously inherited the resilience that helped his father survive twelve months of labor in the dismal Blue Ridge Tunnel.[185]

Over in the Shenandoah Valley, Hannah, former enslaved housekeeper for Blue Ridge Railroad vendor Sampson Pelter, refreshed her life after the war's end. She married Robert Harden, a farm laborer at least six years her senior. Initially, they lived in Mount Sidney, more than sixteen miles north of Pelter's Waynesboro house. Let us hope she felt comforted by the distance from her previous place of bondage and relief when Pelter died in 1865.[186]

Hannah Harden's gravestone, Fairview Cemetery, Waynesboro, Virginia. *Mackenzie Carlsson, 2019.*

By 1870, Hannah's oldest sons, John and Junius, had moved away. Twelve-year-old Abraham remained with his mother and Robert Harden for a while, as did her two grown daughters, Amanda and Sallie, both of whom used the surname of Harden. The identity of their father is unknown, but they were of the right age to be Pelter's children by Hannah Harden. Pelter bequeathed his white daughter only five dollars. His contempt for her, his wife and her niece easily matches the omission of Hannah Harden's daughters, if they were his offspring, in his will.[187]

It seems that none of Hannah's sons took possession of the land they inherited when their father died. In a chancery court case that sputtered on from 1882 through 1890, Joseph, one of Pelter's white sons, claimed that John, Junius and Abraham Pelter owed him about $400. Joseph maintained that the debt was a lien on their inherited property and that the land belonged to him. Existing court records are inconclusive about the outcome of the case.[188]

James Williams's marriage to a woman he later called a "wench" was unsuccessful. "I soon found out this woman was no good," he remembered, "so when we were free I paid no more attention to her." Aside from their two children, the most valuable result of their marriage may have been the slip of paper that William Jarman filled out giving Williams permission to wed her. Slaveholders often listed dates of birth for slaves in family bibles, daybooks and even endpapers of cookbooks. But few freed people had access to a document they could use as a birth certificate. The paper, in effect, confirmed Williams's official existence as a human being, and he treasured it.[189]

Beginning life anew in Augusta County, Williams worked at an iron ore furnace near Sherando Lake. Originally called Shaw's Furnace, it became Whistler's Furnace, named for northerners who owned the enterprise. They employed him for about eighteen years. During this time, Williams married twice. Both wives died. The two unions produced eight children.

Whistler's Furnace was renamed Mount Torry Furnace. It operated until 1884. *Paul Collinge, 2019.*

In 1893, he married—for the fourth and last time—a thirty-four-year-old woman named Sarah.[190]

That same year, a local Mennonite minister sold to James Williams, for one dollar, seven and a half acres east of the South River and north of Waynesboro. The land was off what was then a dirt road to the small settlement of Crimora. Here, Williams built a three-room, one-and-a-half-story cabin where he could farm, chop wood and sometimes indulge in a finger of whiskey. Except for one trip to visit a son in Pennsylvania, occasional church attendance and weekly walks to a small grocery store, he seldom left his farm. The cabin was his and Sarah's refuge for decades.[191]

SERVILE INSURRECTION

The fate of white men who provided or used slave labor on the Blue Ridge Railroad is worth a look. This is especially true for those connected with the University of Virginia, which has told only a heroic version of their histories until recently. Too old for combat in the Confederate army, Thomas Jefferson Randolph received an honorary commission as colonel, and he remained in the South during the conflict. According to a man formerly enslaved at Monticello, Randolph was living in near poverty one year after the war ended. He had lost $80,000 by supporting the Confederacy and owned only his land and a blind mule. Described by the freedman as "proud and haughty," Randolph bitterly blamed his problems on Northerners.[192]

"Southern abolitionism was peaceful reform," Randolph wrote in an unsent letter, "addressed to the white population of the slave states. Northern abolitionism was revolution, addressed to the slave: its means servile insurrection and civil war."[193]

In other words, Randolph believed that passage of his 1832 resolution for the gradual abolition of slavery—written by a Southern white delegate and presented to an audience of other Southern white delegates—could have avoided the Civil War. It was a grandiose interpretation. Even if the resolution had passed in Virginia, few, if any, of the other slaveholding states would have followed suit. Randolph's statement also ignored the sacrifices that northern black and white abolitionists made while helping slaves escape, as well as the deaths of freedmen who fought for the Union.

Randolph's low opinion of Northern abolitionism contrasted sharply with his high opinion of his failed resolution, which he sported as if it were a medal for years after the war ended. He was, he wrote in 1874, the "only man south of the Potomac, who ever had the temerity to present to a legislative body, a distinct proposition for the manumission of the colored race."[194]

Fighting for the Confederacy, John Singleton Mosby led the eponymous Mosby's Rangers on repeated raids in Northern Virginia. Charles Carter continued his work as a physician during the war and died in 1867. When George Custer and his Union troops rode triumphantly through Charlottesville in March 1865, Socrates Maupin joined other faculty at the foot of a hill near the university's Rotunda. Waving a flag of truce, the group asked that the general spare the institution from destruction, which he did. After the Confederate surrender at Appomattox, Maupin held a meeting for university faculty at his house. Most agreed they were under no obligation to assist the people they had held in slavery.[195]

Of the white Blue Ridge Railroad and Virginia Central Railroad men with no University of Virginia connections, only Charles Ellet—with fatal results—landed on the right side of the war. A loyal transplanted Virginian, he was a more loyal Unionist. In letters to Union generals and to President

Chesapeake and Ohio train steaming east of Greenwood, Virginia, on what were Thomas Jefferson Randolph's sections, 1948. *Photographer J.I. Kelly, C&O Historical Society.*

Abraham Lincoln after the conflict began, he offered his engineering experience, hoping he could disable Virginia's railroads. These included the one going "westwardly," he wrote, "to the mountains"—the very line for which he had designed the temporary track eight years earlier. The secretary of war ignored his suggestion but finally heeded his warnings about the need for steamboat rams. In 1862, Ellet led a fleet of rams up the Mississippi River, where a Confederate shot him above the knee at the Battle of Memphis. Ellet expired from his wound two weeks later. His heartbroken wife died shortly thereafter. They were buried in the same grave.[196]

Claudius Crozet died at the home of his daughter and son-in-law in Chesterfield County, Virginia, in 1864. They buried him, with no gravestone, next to his wife and two children in Richmond's Shockoe Hill Cemetery. One of the founders of the Virginia Military Institute, Crozet was reinterred on the school's grounds in 1942. A marker was erected six years later.[197]

William P. Jarman's fortunes took a catastrophic fall between 1860 and 1870. Before the war, his combined assets were valued at $24,900. His father, Thomas Jarman, died around 1868 and cut William—his oldest son—out

George Farrow's grave in a private cemetery at the former Brooksville plantation. *Brian Gallagher, 2016.*

of his will. This may be why William Jarman owned no land in 1870 and his personal estate was worth a mere $500.[198]

Midway through the war, George Farrow sold almost all of the fifteen hundred acres of land that he had accumulated at his Brooksville plantation since 1848. In August 1865, he applied for a pardon for "taking part in the late rebellion against the Government of the United States," as the form stated. The approved application noted that Farrow's assets were still worth more than $20,000. Part of this leftover money was profit made from his Blue Ridge Railroad dealings, including rental of slave labor to the state. Farrow had little time left to enjoy the remaining wealth. He died of heart disease in 1867. His widow applied to the Southern Claims Commission in 1879 for loss of property during the war, but the commission members disallowed her evidence.[199]

9

1939–2008

I'LL TELL YOU STRAIGHT

On a brisk November afternoon in 1939, a visitor climbed the rickety porch steps of James Williams's Augusta County cabin near Crimora. Louis Spilman, editor of the Waynesboro *News Virginian*, had arrived to interview the ninety-nine-year-old. Williams welcomed him, as do most elderly people who appreciate an audience for long-ago stories. The two men sat close to a woodstove for warmth. An oil lamp provided light. In the fading hours of dusk, Spilman asked questions and listened. Sarah Williams, ninety-one and deaf, may have been a silent witness to the conversation.

Spilman was curious about Williams's advanced age and especially interested in his personal habits. "Do you drink liquor, Uncle Jim?" he asked. "Do you smoke or chew? Do you watch your diet?"[200]

Williams began his answers with an honest, "Well, I'll tell you straight now that you're askin' me." He had not been drunk in sixty years. He gave up smoking but chewed tobacco. He could eat anything put in front of him, even a big dish of cucumbers just before bedtime. Then, in a demonstration of good health, he performed a few knee-to-shoulder jig steps and showed Spilman how he chopped wood.[201]

Examined through a 1930s lens, Louis Spilman was a respectful interviewer. The full-page profile he published in the newspaper a few weeks later described Williams's conversation as "deliberate, enthusiastic, convincing, sincere, and downright fascinating."[202]

James Williams, 1939.
Cover of sheet music for
"Ole Uncle Jim." *W.R.
Humphries, photographer,
author's collection.*

Williams was an equally respectful yet cautious interviewee. He spoke kindly of almost every white person he mentioned, excepting the slaveholder he had overheard at Mudwall Tavern. No one can tell now if Spilman prompted Williams with loaded questions meant to produce positive responses about white people, or if the newspaperman edited out answers unacceptable for white readers. In any case, Spilman may have paraphrased some of Williams's answers.[203]

James Williams would have learned that self-censorship was the best policy while in the presence of a white person. In 1939, the year of his interview, Virginia was midway through a terrifying reign of eighty to one hundred lynchings that lasted from 1877 to 1950. Though none are documented for Augusta County, mobs lynched four black men in three counties bordering Augusta. Williams surely heard about these ghastly acts of violence and instinctively protected himself while speaking with Spilman. Fountain Hughes, a former slave born in Charlottesville, expressed such restraint well:[204] "You wasn't no more than a dog to some of them in them days. You wasn't treated as good as they treat dogs now. But still I didn't like to talk about it. Because it makes, makes people feel bad you know. Uh, I, I could say a whole lot I don't like to say. And I won't say a whole lot more."[205]

Looked at with a more enlightened, twenty-first-century lens, Louis Spilman's interview was a failure. He would have known that many members of his reading audience were fans of *Gone with the Wind*, the wildly successful Civil War novel published three years earlier. Appealing to those readers, he larded much of his article with Lost Cause romanticism. "Uncle Jim," he wrote, "exudes the hospitality of the Old South of ante-bellum days so ingrained in his heart and soul when he served first in the home of Captain Thomas Jarman and then later in the home of Captain Tom's son, William, to whom Uncle Jim was given by his first master."[206]

James Williams was no servant. He had been a chattel slave. Thomas and William Jarman were no one's masters. They were enslavers. And let us give the mother of Williams credit for his polite manners and calm demeanor. If he had a "consistently happy, pleasant outlook on life," as Louis Spilman wrote, it was she who would have encouraged those qualities in her son, not the people who exploited his labor and whipped him. Spilman published his profile of James Williams one week before the long-awaited premiere of the *Gone with the Wind* film. In the book and on screen, white residents of the fictional Tara plantation had their cherished Mammy and loyal Big Sam. Spilman's article provided his white readers with their very own, beloved Uncle Jim.[207]

Sarah Williams died at age 92 in January 1941. James Williams joined her in death one month later at age 102. (See appendix 2.) Both were buried in a cemetery adjoining the John Wesley United African Methodist Episcopal Church, located just north of Crimora. African Americans founded the congregation sometime in the 1870s and first held services at a schoolhouse known as Belvidere School No. 25 (col.).[208]

The school no longer stands, nor does the church building that congregants constructed next to it in 1892. The nearby graveyard is now hidden in tangled undergrowth and trees. As of the year 2000, only seven inscribed stones for freed slaves and the children of freed slaves survived—none for Sarah or James Williams—along with many graves marked by small, roughly rounded fieldstones. In 2008, drivers of a Bush Hog and a tractor cleared brush away from utility poles and all but destroyed the Wesley/Belvidere Cemetery.

Death certificate for James Williams, 1941. Note that the coroner listed his burial place on line eighteen as "Belvadier." *Dale Brumfield.*

In doing so, they demolished the only known burial place for an enslaved laborer on Blue Ridge Railroad tracks.[209]

Construction of a narrow, paved lane also intruded on the cemetery property at some point. More graves might lie under the asphalt. A line of head-to-toe, coffin-shaped depressions parallels the lane. As is common in older African American cemeteries, families planted periwinkle ground cover, spiky yucca plants and flowering shrubs near the graves. Though the coffins may have been moved or destroyed, the plants create distinctive markers for people buried in the cemetery long ago.[210]

Every enslaved person whose labor contributed to the Blue Ridge Railroad had a heart full of memories—of the railroad construction and Civil War, of emancipation and a post-slavery life. Time and lack of documents have obscured their recollections, leaving a jagged hole in the railroad's history. But the profile of James Williams survives, and for that we must be grateful—with

Restoration of the Blue Ridge Tunnel included a wider stone parapet above the portal and a more level floor for hikers and bicyclists. *Jim Kauffman, 2019.*

reservations—to Louis Spilman. More first-person accounts or handed-down family stories are waiting for discovery. Until they surface, James Williams's lone voice speaks eloquently for the hundreds of enslaved people who toiled along the Blue Ridge Railroad and in the Blue Ridge Tunnel.

EPILOGUE

In 1971, the Virginia section of the American Society of Civil Engineers (ASCE) nominated the Blue Ridge Tunnel for recognition as a National Historic Engineering Landmark. As proof that the passage should join this premier list of outstanding structures, they submitted numerous documents to the national ASCE in New York. These included pages of historical background, book excerpts and recommendation letters. The engineers noted that, as the first tunnel through the Virginia Blue Ridge Mountains, the Blue Ridge Tunnel was a "landmark contribution in the development of the United States" and its "national transportation and commerce."[211]

Virginia's civil engineers further declared that Claudius Crozet's work "promoted the progress of the Middle West by providing an easy emigration to that territory and a quick outlet to the sea for its products." The Smithsonian Institution agreed. "Without any doubt," wrote a curator, "the Blue Ridge tunnel is an important one, fully deserving of CE [civil engineer] landmark status."[212]

After a painstaking selection process, the national ASCE awarded the Blue Ridge Tunnel its landmark designation in 1976. During an annual meeting held at Natural Bridge, Virginia, a national ASCE official presented an eight-by-eighteen-inch bronze plaque to the nominators. "National Historic Civil Engineering Landmark" was emblazoned on the top. The brightly polished words "Crozet Tunnel" appeared at the bottom. An insignia in the center enclosed the phrase "American Society of Civil Engineers Founded 1852."[213]

As with the inscribed stone tablets that once topped portals at the Greenwood and Blue Ridge Tunnels, the bronze plaque made no mention of laborers. The nomination papers managed to describe the Irish in condescending terms but completely omitted mention of enslaved people whose labor contributed to the Blue Ridge Tunnel. One of the documents called the tunnel a "miracle." I expand that word to include the entire Blue Ridge Railroad, as no railroad tunnel can operate without a railroad. Invisible behind this miraculous achievement were enslaved laborers. They, too, made "landmark contributions in the development of the United States."[214]

Despite efforts to locate the 1976 bronze plaque, it remains lost. Perhaps this book can serve as a replacement with the long overdue recognition that was absent on the original. Names known or unknown, it is time we salute the enslaved men, women and boys who were forced participants in a memorable chapter of the American story.

TRANSCRIPTION OF THE FARROW-HANSBROUGH CONTRACT

23rd Dec. 1853
Recd. 5. January 1854.
5. January 1854. approved.
Blue Ridge Railroad
Contract for the hire of Negroes
Articles of Agreement

Entered into this Twenty-third day of December in the year Eighteen hundred and fifty three between the Board of Public works, by Claudius Crozet, Engineer of the Blue ridge railroad, of the one part, and George A. Farrow & David Hansbrough, of the other part:

Witness, that the said Geo. A Farrow & David Hansbrough agree to furnish from forty to fifty able bodied negro men to be employed at work on the Blue ridge railroad and Tunnel, chiefly under the management of Kelly and Larguey, the contractors for the main Tunnel, who are to examine and receive or refuse such negroes, according to their judgement of the fitness of each to perform the work he is intended for.[215]

And for the Services of said negroes, the Board of Public works agree to pay monthly at the rate of One dollar and twelve and a half cents ($1.12½) per day, each negro shall have been at work during the month, according to the payroll to be exhibited at the end of every month to the Engineer.

And it is, moreover, agreed between the parties that, for the purpose of overlooking and attending to said negroes, on either side of the mountain, the said Farrow and Hansbrough shall select and furnish two white men whose duty it shall be, under the direction of the agents of the railroad, to superintend the conduct and work of said negroes and attend to their wants, keeping carefully the regular check roll of their days' work. The said superintendents shall receive for their services each at the rate of thirty-five ($35) per month.

If, in addition to the above, blacksmiths are hired from the aforesaid Farrow and Hansbrough, their hire shall be one dollar and forty cents, for each, per day of work.

Moreover, it is understood that in case any of said negroes should be injured by any accident resulting immediately from his employment on the work, the Board of Public works agree to pay the damage done to said negro or negroes, by valuation of umpires chosen for the purpose by the parties; each party to this contract choosing one.

And it is farther distinctly agreed and understood that said negroes shall not be employed in loading or blasting on said work.

Finally, it is agreed that the said negroes shall be hired to the Board of Public works during the whole of the year Eighteen hundred and fifty-four: and, for the faithful performance of this part of the present contract, the said Geo. A. Farrow and David Hansbrough agree to enter into bond, with satisfactory security, in the sum of three thousand dollars, payable to the Board of Public works.

It is also understood that such parts of the general specification for the Blue ridge railroad, as are applicable to and not conflicting with, the present contract are to be considered as making part of the same.

In witness whereof, Claudius Crozet, Engineer of the Blue ridge railroad has hereunto set his hand & seal; and the said Geo. A. Farrow & David Hansbrough have hereunto set their hands and seals, the day & year first herein written.

Claudius Crozet L.S.

George A. Farrow L.S.

David Hansbrough L.S.[216]

WILLIAMS OBITUARIES

"Uncle Jim" Williams' Wife, Age 93, Succumbs"

Mrs. Sarah Williams, age 93, wife of "Uncle Jim" Williams, 102, died last night at midnight. Her death was very sudden.

Funeral services will be held at Belvedere sometime Sunday. The funeral procession will meet at Belvedere. Her body will be at the Wilberger Funeral Home until the time for the funeral.

She is survived by her husband, Jim Williams of Crimora; three brothers, Will Darcus, Sam Darcus, and Luther Darcus, and one daughter, Mary Brown, of New York.[217]

"Ex-Slave, 102, Is Found Dead. Funeral Arrangements Not Yet Completed"

"Uncle Jim" Williams, of near Crimora, ex-slave who celebrated his 102nd birthday last August 28th, was found dead in bed at his home yesterday where he had lived alone since the passing of his wife on January 21 at the age of 93.

Body was taken to the Wilberger Funeral Home where it will remain until funeral arrangements can be completed. Death was attributed to old age.

Until recently Uncle Jim had been well and active. He had chopped his own fire wood, looked after his own cooking, and tended his own household work. Neighbors missed the sound of his axe at the woodpile and started the investigation which discovered his body.

"Uncle Jim's" survivors include a daughter, Mrs. Alice Rhodes, of Waynesboro; a stepson, Ernest Brown, of Elizabeth, New Jersey; a son, Jack Johnson, of Waynesboro; and several grandchildren.[218]

"News of Our Colored Folks"

Funeral for aged "Uncle Jim" Williams of Crimora was held from the John Wessley [*sic*] M.E. Church at 8 p.m., Sunday. Feb. 21st. Rev. C.H. Harris, Pastor of the Shiloh Baptist Church, Waynesboro, assisted by the Rev. George W. Steward, pastor of the Union Baptist Church, Waynesboro, officiated. A very large gathering consisting largely of white persons assembled to pay their last tribute of respect to the 102-year-old man. His 93-year-old wife, preceded him to the grave just four weeks, prior. Among those attending from Waynesboro were, Houston Murray, Sr., Huey Murray, Sr., Hurley Williams, Miss Irene Murray and Huey Murray, Jr.[219]

APPENDIX 3

SECTIONS, CONTRACTORS AND LABOR FORCE

Section	Contractors	Year	Laborers
1	John Kelly and John Larguey:	1850–53	Irish, local whites
	Blue Ridge Tunnel, 1,000 feet beyond	1854–56	Irish, enslaved, local whites
	east portal approach and east side embankment	1857–58	Irish, local
2	Mordecai Sizer	1850–52	Irish, enslaved
	George A. Farrow	1852	Enslaved, local whites
	Robert P. Smith	1853–54	Enslaved, local whites
	John Kelly	1858	Irish, local
3	Mordecai Sizer	1850–52	Irish, enslaved
	George A. Farrow	1852	Enslaved
	Robert P. Smith	1852–54	Enslaved

Section	Contractors	Year	Laborers
4	Mordecai Sizer	1850–52	Irish, enslaved
	Hugh S. Gallaher and Samuel McElroy	1852–55	Enslaved
	John Kelly	1858	Irish, local whites
5	John Kelly: Brooksville Tunnel	1850–56	Irish, local whites
	John Kelly: Kelly's Cut	1850–54, 1856–58	Irish, local whites
	James Goodloe: Kelly's Cut	1856	Enslaved
6	John Kelly: Greenwood Tunnel	1850–53	Irish
7	Thomas Jefferson Randolph and Christopher Valentine	1850–52	Enslaved
	Robert F. Harris: brick culvert	1852	Unknown
8	Thomas Jefferson Randolph and Christopher Valentine	1850–52	Enslaved
9	Walker and Co. (Walker and Gallaher)	1851–53	Enslaved, local whites
	Gallaher and Co.	1854	Enslaved, local whites
10	Hugh L. Gallaher and Co.	1851	Enslaved, local whites
11	Timothy Ives and Co. (Ives, Walker and Gallaher)	1851–54	Enslaved
12	Daniel Collins and Thomas Baskins	1851–52	Likely Irish
	Jonathan Browning	1853	Unknown
13	William S. Carter and Charles Goodman	1852	Enslaved
14	William S. Carter and Charles Goodman	1852	Enslaved
15	Elisha Melton and Stapleton Dabney Gooch	1851–52	Enslaved

Section	Contractors	Year	Laborers
16	Clement Lukens and James Wallace	1851–52	Likely Irish
	Hugh L. Gallaher and Samuel McElroy	1852	Enslaved
	William M. Sclater and Robert Richardson	1853	Enslaved
	William S. Carter: ballasting	1852–53	Enslaved
	Robert P. Smith: trimming and ballasting	1853	Enslaved
	W.B. Phillips and John R. Holmes: culvert	1851–52	Possibly enslaved
	N.S. Carpenter: track layer	1854	Irish

APPENDIX 4

NAMES OF ENSLAVED LABORERS

Enslaved Laborer	Slaveholders and Their Locations	Dates of Enslaved Labor	Task and Location of Slave Labor	Rate of Pay to Slaveholder
Abe (also Abraham)	David Hansbrough Brooksville area Western Albemarle Co.	02/1854–12/1854 01/1855, 12/1855 01/1856–06/1856	Blacksmith Blue Ridge Tunnel	$1.30–1.42 ½/day
Abell, Harry	George A. Farrow Brooksville area Western Albemarle Co.	01/1854	Floorer Blue Ridge Tunnel	$1.12 ½ /day
Abell, Oddy	George A. Farrow Brooksville area Western Albemarle Co.	01/1854	Floorer Blue Ridge Tunnel	$1.12 ½ /day
Adam	William Warwick Western Albemarle Co.	01/1854– 01/01/1855	Contingent tasks Blue Ridge Railroad	$150/year
Addison	William H. Harris Albemarle Co.	04/01/1854– 01/01/1855	Contingent tasks Blue Ridge Railroad	$125.00
Anderson	J. Yancey Albemarle Co.	01/1854– 01/01/1855	Contingent tasks Blue Ridge Railroad	$130.00/ year

Enslaved Laborer	Slaveholders and Their Locations	Dates of Enslaved Labor	Task and Location of Slave Labor	Rate of Pay to Slaveholder
Andrew	Possibly James Burnley Albemarle Co.	03/1852	Fireman Virginia Central Railroad Woodville (now Ivy) Depot	$0.80/day
Andy	G.A. (George Alexander) Bruce Waynesboro, VA	1851	Delivered cornmeal Blue Ridge Railroad	Not applicable
Armistead	Elizabeth Powell Mechum's Depot area Western Albemarle Co.	01/1854–01/1855	Contingent tasks Blue Ridge Railroad	$150.00/ year Payable quarterly
Arthur	William Ramsay Western Albemarle Co.	12/1854	Floorer Blue Ridge Tunnel	$1.12 ½ /day
Barns, Thomas (also Tom, also Barnes)	David Hansbrough Brooksville area Western Albemarle Co.	01/1854–11/1854 01/1855, 12/1855 01/1856–06/1856	Floorer and blacksmith Blue Ridge Tunnel	$1.12 ½ – $1.42 ½ /day
Ben	Alfred D. Mosby Albemarle Co.	07/17/1854– 01/01/1855	Contingent tasks Blue Ridge Railroad	$65.00
Benjamin	William Ramsay Western Albemarle Co.	12/1854	Floorer Blue Ridge Tunnel	$1.12 ½ /day
Bob	Dr. Charles Carter Charlottesville, VA	01/1854– 01/01/1855	Contingent tasks Blue Ridge Railroad	$150.00 /year
Bob	Thomas W. Williams Formerly the Williams brothers' Yellow House "slave pen" Washington, D.C.	01/1854– 01/01/1855	Contingent tasks Blue Ridge Railroad	$150.00 /year
Bracket, Remus	Dr. Charles Carter Charlottesville, VA	01/1854– 01/01/1855	Contingent tasks Blue Ridge Railroad	$150.00 /year

Enslaved Laborer	Slaveholders and Their Locations	Dates of Enslaved Labor	Task and Location of Slave Labor	Rate of Pay to Slaveholder
Bracket, Romulus	Dr. Charles Carter Charlottesville, VA	01/1854– 01/01/1855	Contingent tasks Blue Ridge Railroad	$150.00 /year
Bruce, Len (also Lynn, Lenn)	George A. Farrow Brooksville area Western Albemarle Co.	01/1854, 02/1854 04/1854–12/1854	Floorer Blue Ridge Tunnel	$1.12 ½ /day
Caleb	Andrew Woods Woodville (now Ivy) area Western Albemarle Co.	01/09/1854– 01/01/1855	Contingent tasks Blue Ridge Railroad	$150.00
Carter, Samuel	George A. Farrow Brooksville area Western Albemarle Co.	01/1854, 02/1854 04/1854–12/1854	Floorer Blue Ridge Tunnel	$1.12½ /day
Carter, Wesley	David Hansbrough Brooksville area Western Albemarle Co.	01/1854–12/1854 01/1855–03/1855	Floorer Blue Ridge Tunnel	$1.12 ½ /day
Champ, Joe (also Joseph)	George A. Farrow Brooksville area Western Albemarle Co.	01/1854–12/1854	Floorer Blue Ridge Tunnel	$1.12 ½ /day
Coy	George W. Kinsolving Mechum's Depot area Western Albemarle Co.	01/01/1854– 01/01/1855	Contingent tasks Blue Ridge Railroad	$150.00/ year
Curtis	Possibly James Burnley Albemarle Co.	03/1852	Fireman Virginia Central Railroad, Woodville (now Ivy) Depot	$0.80/day
Dabney	Socrates Maupin University of Virginia	01/1854– 01/01/1855	Contingent tasks Blue Ridge Railroad	$150.00/ year
Davenport, David	George A. Farrow Brooksville area Western Albemarle Co.	01/1854–12/1854	Floorer Blue Ridge Tunnel	$1.12 ½ /day

Enslaved Laborer	Slaveholders and Their Locations	Dates of Enslaved Labor	Task and Location of Slave Labor	Rate of Pay to Slaveholder
David	Possibly James Burnley Albemarle Co.	03/1852	Fireman Virginia Central Railroad Woodville (now Ivy) Depot	$0.80/day
David	William H. Harris Albemarle Co.	04/01/1854– 01/1855	Contingent tasks Blue Ridge Railroad	$125.00
Dennis	Unknown	03/1852	Train hand Virginia Central Railroad Woodville (now Ivy) Depot	$0.80/day
Dennis	J. Yancey Albemarle Co.	01/01/1854– 01/01/1855	Contingent tasks Blue Ridge Railroad	$130.00/ year
Dick	Unknown	03/1852	Train hand Virginia Central Railroad Woodville (now Ivy) Depot	$0.80/day
Elias	George A. Farrow Brooksville area Western Albemarle Co.	04/1854–12/1854	Floorer Blue Ridge Tunnel	$1.12 ½ /day
Ellick	James Burnley Albemarle Co.	03/1852	Fireman Virginia Central Railroad Woodville (now Ivy) Depot	$0.80/day
Ellick	John S. Cocke Western Albemarle Co.	04/01/1852– 04/12/1852	Unknown	$1.00/day
Ellis	Alfred D. Mosby Albemarle Co.	07/17/1854– 01/01/1855	Contingent tasks Blue Ridge Railroad	$65.00
Fleming	George A. Farrow Brooksville area Western Albemarle Co.	01/1854–12/1854	Floorer Blue Ridge Tunnel	$1.00– $1.12 ½ /day

Enslaved Laborer	Slaveholders and Their Locations	Dates of Enslaved Labor	Task and Location of Slave Labor	Rate of Pay to Slaveholder
Fountain	William Amos Maupin by Addison Maupin, brother and executor of his estate Albemarle Co.	01/01/1854– 01/01/1855	Contingent tasks Blue Ridge Railroad	$150.00/ year Payable quarterly
Gallon, Albert	George A. Farrow Brooksville area Western Albemarle Co.	01/1854 payroll	Floorer Blue Ridge Tunnel	$1.12 ½ /day
George	Hiram Via Albemarle Co.	01/09/1854– 01/01/1855	Contingent tasks Blue Ridge Railroad	$150.00/ year
George	Dr. Charles Carter Charlottesville, VA	01/1854–01/1855	Contingent tasks Blue Ridge Railroad	$150.00/ year
George	William H. Harris Albemarle Co.	04/01/1854– 01/01/1855	Contingent tasks Blue Ridge Railroad	$125.00
George	James M. Bowen Greenwood, Western Albemarle Co.	1855, 1857	Delivery of steel bars, wick, fuse Blue Ridge Tunnel Delivery of freight Blue Ridge Railroad	Unknown
Goliah	Margaret Dawson by William Graves, her guardian Mechum's Depot area Western Albemarle Co.	01/1854– 01/01/1855	Contingent tasks Blue Ridge Railroad	$150.00/ year Payable quarterly
Groves, Henry	George A. Farrow Brooksville area Western Albemarle Co.	01/1854, 02/1854 04/1854–12/1854	Floorer Blue Ridge Tunnel	$1.12 ½ /day
Hailstock, Reuben (also Ailstock)	George A. Farrow Brooksville area Western Albemarle Co.	01/1854–12/1854	Floorer Blue Ridge Tunnel	$1.12 ½ /day

Enslaved Laborer	Slaveholders and Their Locations	Dates of Enslaved Labor	Task and Location of Slave Labor	Rate of Pay to Slaveholder
Harden, Hannah	Sampson Pelter Waynesboro, VA	Estimated 1840s–1865	Housekeeper Pelter mansion	Not applicable
Hartshorn, Albert	George A. Farrow Brooksville area Western Albemarle Co.	01/1854–12/1854	Floorer Blue Ridge Tunnel	$1.12 ½ /day
Hartshorn, Lewis (also Louis)	George A. Farrow Brooksville area Western Albemarle Co.	01/1854–12/1854	Floorer Blue Ridge Tunnel	$1.12 ½ /day
Henderson	Austin G. Shelton Mechum's Depot area Western Albemarle Co.	01/01/1854– 01/01/1855	Contingent tasks Blue Ridge Railroad	$150.00/ year
Henry	Ira Maupin Mechum's Depot area Western Albemarle Co.	01/01/1854– 01/01/1855	Contingent tasks Blue Ridge Railroad	$150.00/ year
Henry, boy	William H. Harris Albemarle Co.	04/01/1854– 01/01/1855	Contingent tasks Blue Ridge Railroad	$50.00
Horace	Thomas W. Williams Formerly Williams brothers' Yellow House "slave pen," Washington, D.C.	01/01/1854– 01/01/1855	Contingent tasks Blue Ridge Railroad	$150.00/ year
Jacob	William Rothwell Mechum's Depot area Western Albemarle Co.	01/01/1854– 01/01/1855	Contingent tasks Blue Ridge Railroad	$145.00
James	Chapman [C.?] Maupin Albemarle Co.	01/01/1854– 01/01/1855	Contingent tasks Blue Ridge Railroad	$150.00/ year
James	Warrick Woods Brooksville area Western Albemarle Co.	01/01/1854– 01/01/1855	Contingent tasks Blue Ridge Railroad	$150.00/ year
Jefferson	Thomas W. Williams Formerly Williams brothers' Yellow House "slave pen," Washington, D.C.	01/09/1854– 01/01/1855	Contingent tasks Blue Ridge Railroad	$90.00/ year

Enslaved Laborer	Slaveholders and Their Locations	Dates of Enslaved Labor	Task and Location of Slave Labor	Rate of Pay to Slaveholder
Jefferson	William Woods Albemarle Co.	01/01/1854– 01/01/1855	Contingent tasks Blue Ridge Railroad	$150.00/ year
Jerry	James Garland Woodville (now Ivy) area Western Albemarle Co.	01/01/1854– 04/06/1854	Contingent tasks Blue Ridge Railroad	$150.00/ year
Jesse	Peter A. Woods, William H. Jones, trustees Unknown	01/09/1854– 01/01/1855	Contingent tasks Blue Ridge Railroad	$135.00/ year
Joe	J. Yancey Albemarle Co.	01/01/1854– 01/01/1855	Contingent tasks Blue Ridge Railroad	$130.00/ year
John, "free boy"	Unknown	03/1852	Unknown Virginia Central Railroad Woodville (now Ivy) Depot	1 month at $15.00
Johnson	Chapman [C.?] Maupin Albemarle Co.	01/01/1854– 01/01/1855	Contingent tasks Blue Ridge Railroad	$150.00/ year
Jones, Henry	George A. Farrow Brooksville area Western Albemarle Co.	01/1854–06/1854 08/1854–12/1854	Floorer Blue Ridge Tunnel	$1.00– $1.12 ½ /day
Leuvil	John Woods Woodville (now Ivy) area Western Albemarle Co.	01/01/1854– 01/01/1855	Contingent tasks Blue Ridge Railroad	$150.00/ year
Lewis	William Graves Mechum's Depot area Western Albemarle Co.	01/01/1854– 01/01/1855	Contingent tasks Blue Ridge Railroad	$150.00/ year Payable quarterly
Lewis	William Tilman Mechum's Depot area Western Albemarle Co.	01/01/1854– 01/01/1855	Contingent tasks Blue Ridge Railroad	$150.00/ year

Enslaved Laborer	Slaveholders and Their Locations	Dates of Enslaved Labor	Task and Location of Slave Labor	Rate of Pay to Slaveholder
Lewis, first name possibly Aaron	Unknown	1853, 1854	Delivery of 4 gallons tar Blue Ridge Railroad Delivery of shingles, tar Blue Ridge Railroad	Not applicable
Macajah	Andrew M. Woods Woodville (now Ivy) area Western Albemarle Co.	01/09/1854– 01/01/1855	Contingent tasks Blue Ridge Railroad	$150.00
Mickums, Robert (also Bob)	David Hansbrough Brooksville area Western Albemarle Co.	01/1854–12/1854 01/1855–03/1855 12/1855 01/1856–06/1856	Blacksmith Blue Ridge Tunnel	$1.30– $1.45½ /day
Nables, Jordan	George A. Farrow Brooksville area Western Albemarle Co.	01/1854, 02/1854 04/1854–12/1854	Floorer Blue Ridge Tunnel	$1.12 ½ /day
Pacing, Larus	George A. Farrow Brooksville area Western Albemarle Co.	01/1854, 03/1854	Floorer Blue Ridge Tunnel	$1.12 ½/day
Paldox, Don	George A. Farrow Brooksville area Western Albemarle Co.	01/1854	Floorer Blue Ridge Tunnel	$1.12 ½ /day
Phil	Unknown	1853	Blacksmith Sections 2, 3, and/or 16	$37.50/ month
Powers, Randal (also Randall, Randolph)	George A. Farrow Brooksville area Western Albemarle Co.	01/1854, 02/1854 04/1854–08/1854	Floorer Blue Ridge Tunnel	$1.12 ½ /day
Robert	David Hansbrough Brooksville area Western Albemarle Co.	1856	Delivery of picks, hammer handles Blue Ridge Railroad	Not applicable

Enslaved Laborer	Slaveholders and Their Locations	Dates of Enslaved Labor	Task and Location of Slave Labor	Rate of Pay to Slaveholder
Sam	William Withrow, Jr. Augusta Co.	1853	Delivery of 4 ½ gallons tar Blue Ridge Railroad	Not applicable
Sam	John Maupin White Hall Western Albemarle Co.	Likely 01/1854– 05/25/1854	Contingent tasks Blue Ridge Railroad	Not applicable
Scipio	Alfred D. Mosby Albemarle Co.	07/17/1854– 01/01/1855	Contingent tasks Blue Ridge Railroad	$65.00
Shanklin, William	George A. Farrow Brooksville area Western Albemarle Co.	01/1854, 02/1854 04/1854–12/1854	Floorer Blue Ridge Tunnel	$1.12 ½ /day
Sherrod	William King Charlottesville, VA	04/23/1849– 12/14/1849	Likely portage Blue Ridge Railroad	$0.50/day = $102.00
Spears, William (also Spiers, Speers)	George A. Farrow Brooksville area Western Albemarle Co.	01/1854, 02/1854 04/1854–12/1854	Floorer Blue Ridge Tunnel	$1.00– $1.12 ½ /day
Tandy	Chapman [C.?] Maupin Albemarle Co.	01/01/1854– 01/01/1855	Contingent tasks Blue Ridge Railroad	$150.00/ year
Taylor, Shadrach (also Shadrack)	George A. Farrow Brooksville area Western Albemarle Co.	02/1854–12/1854	Floorer Blue Ridge Tunnel	$1.12 ½ /day
Tilman	Possibly William Tilman Mechum's Depot area Western Albemarle Co.	03/1852	Train hand Virginia Central Railroad Woodville (now Ivy) Depot	$0.80/day
Tom	Vienna Fretwell Mechum's Depot area Western Albemarle Co.	01/01/1854– 01/01/1855	Contingent tasks Blue Ridge Railroad	$150.00/ year

Enslaved Laborer	Slaveholders and Their Locations	Dates of Enslaved Labor	Task and Location of Slave Labor	Rate of Pay to Slaveholder
Tom	Andrew M. Woods Woodville (now Ivy) area Western Albemarle Co.	01/09/1854– 04/06/1854	Contingent tasks Blue Ridge Railroad	$150.00/ year
Unnamed boy	James H. Jarman Mechum's Depot area Western Albemarle Co.	01/01/1854– 01/01/1855	Contingent tasks Blue Ridge Railroad	$50.00/ year
Unnamed man	Robert F. Harris Charlottesville, VA	01/01/1854– 01/01/1855	Contingent tasks Blue Ridge Railroad	$150.00/ year minus doctor fees
Unnamed man	James H. Jarman Mechum's Depot area Western Albemarle Co.	01/01/1854– 01/01/1855	Blacksmith Blue Ridge Railroad	$200.00/ year
Unnamed man	James H. Jarman Mechum's Depot area Western Albemarle Co.	01/01/1854– 01/01/1855	Hand Blue Ridge Railroad	$150.00/ year
Unnamed man	Boarded with Jeremiah Wayland present-day town of Crozet	06/1849	"Servant" Blue Ridge Railroad	2 days at $.050 = $1.00
Unnamed man	William Ramsay Western Albemarle Co.	1852	Delivery of oil Blue Ridge Tunnel	Not applicable
Unnamed men, 2	William Withrow, Jr. Augusta Co.	1851	Delivery of nails, cement Blue Ridge Railroad	Not applicable
Unnamed men, 9	Robert F. Harris Charlottesville, VA	1851	Brick makers Greenwood Tunnel, Blue Ridge Railroad	Unknown
Unnamed men, 12	Charles Ellet Various	1856	Maintenance Virginia Central Railroad temporary track	1 year at $150.00 = $1,800.00

Enslaved Laborer	Slaveholders and Their Locations	Dates of Enslaved Labor	Task and Location of Slave Labor	Rate of Pay to Slaveholder
Unnamed men estimated: 42–72	Mordecai Sizer Prince William Co.	12/1849–1852	Contingent tasks Blue Ridge Railroad Sections 2, 3, 4	Unknown
Unnamed men estimated: 55	Thomas Jefferson Randolph Eastern Albemarle Co. Christopher Valentine Louisa Co.	04/1850–1852	Contingent tasks Blue Ridge Railroad Sections 7, 8	Unknown
Unreadable	Ira Maupin Mechum's Depot area Western Albemarle Co.	01/01/1854– 01/01/1855	Contingent tasks Blue Ridge Railroad	$150.00/ year
Walls, Stephen (also Steven)	George A. Farrow Brooksville area Western Albemarle Co.	01/1854–12/1854	Floorer Blue Ridge Tunnel	$1.12 ½ /day
Wards, Abel	George A. Farrow Brooksville area Western Albemarle Co.	01/1854	Blacksmith Blue Ridge Tunnel	$1.12 ½ /day
Washington	George A. Farrow Brooksville area Western Albemarle Co.	01/1854, 02/1854 04/1854–12/1854	Floorer Blue Ridge Tunnel	$1.12 ½ /day
Watsin [*sic*]	Overton Tillman [*sic*] Mechum's Depot area Western Albemarle Co.	01/01/1854– 01/01/1855	Contingent tasks Blue Ridge Railroad	$150.00/ year
White, Sandy	George A. Farrow Brooksville area Western Albemarle Co.	01/1854–12/1854	Floorer Blue Ridge Tunnel	$1.12 ½ /day
Williams, James	Thomas H. Jarman William P. Jarman White Hall Western Albemarle Co.	1853	Cart boy Blue Ridge Railroad Sections 2 and/ or 3	$50.00/ year estimated

Uncounted Enslaved Laborers	Contractor or Slaveholder	Dates of Labor	Task and Location	Rate of Pay
Number unknown	John S. Cocke Greenwood Western Albemarle Co.	Summer 1850	Portage Blue Ridge Railroad	Unknown
Number unknown	George A. Farrow Brooksville area Western Albemarle Co.	1852	Contingent tasks Blue Ridge Railroad Sections 2, 3	Unknown
Number unknown	Robert P. Smith Brooksville area Western Albemarle Co.	1853–1854	Contingent tasks Blue Ridge Railroad Sections 2, 3,16	Unknown
Number unknown	Hugh L. Gallaher Augusta Co. Samuel McElroy Augusta Co.	1853–1855	Contingent tasks Blue Ridge Railroad Section 4	Unknown
Number unknown	Reuben L. Walker Albemarle Co. Hugh L. Gallaher Augusta Co.	1851–1854	Contingent tasks Blue Ridge Railroad Sections 9, 10, 11	1851: $125.00– $130.00/ man
Number unknown	Hugh L. Gallaher & Co. Augusta Co.	1853–1854	Contingent tasks Blue Ridge Railroad Section 12	Unknown
Number unknown	William S. Carter Green Springs Louisa Co. Charles Goodman Green Springs Louisa Co.	1852–1853	Contingent tasks Blue Ridge Railroad Sections 13,14, 16	Unknown
Number unknown	Stapleton D. Gooch Hanover Co. Elisha Melton Louisa Co.	1851–1852	Contingent tasks Blue Ridge Railroad Section 15	Unknown
Number unknown	William M. Sclater Fluvanna Co. Robert Richardson Fluvanna Co.	1853	Contingent tasks Blue Ridge Railroad Section 16	Unknown

Sources: Blue Ridge Tunnel payrolls, contracts for slave labor, account books and miscellaneous records, Blue Ridge Railroad Papers, Library of Virginia; George Farrow family daybook, private collection; U.S. Census and Slave Schedules, Albemarle County, Virginia, 1850, 1860; Charles Ellet, "The Mountain Top Track" annual report, December 1, 1856; Virginia Central Railroad records, Brock Collection, reel 4590, Library of Virginia; *Waynesboro News Virginian*, December 7, 1939. For a description of contingent tasks, see Claudius Crozet to the Board of Public Works, December 6, 1853, Blue Ridge Railroad Papers, Library of Virginia.

NOTES

Introduction

1. William C. Allen, *History of Slave Laborers in the Construction of the United States Capitol* (Washington, D.C.: Office of the Architect of the Capitol, 2005); Mark Holmberg, "18th-Century Vouchers Show Slaves Built Virginia Capitol," *Richmond Times Dispatch*, July 29, 2016, 3.
2. Gene Zechmeister, "Funding the University of Virginia," Monticello and the University of Virginia in Charlottesville, November 2, 2011, https://www.monticello.org; Brendan Wolfe, "Slavery at the University of Virginia," Encyclopedia Virginia, last modified February 2, 2016, https://www.encyclopediavirginia.org.
3. Ibid.
4. David W. Coffey, "Into the Valley of Virginia: The 1852 Travel Account of Curran Swaim," *Virginia Cavalcade* 39, no. 4 (Spring 1990): 17.
5. Claudius Crozet to President and Directors of the Blue Ridge Railroad, November 30, 1849, Blue Ridge Railroad Papers (hereafter cited as BRP), Library of Virginia, Richmond, VA.
6. Claudius Crozet to Board of Public Works (hereafter cited as BPW), January 10, 1857, BRP; Crozet to James Brown Jr., June 18, 1850, BRP; Crozet to the Blue Ridge Railroad Office, January 15, 1851, BRP; Coy Barefoot, *The Corner: A History of Student Life at the University of Virginia* (Charlottesville, VA: Howell Press, 2002), 34.
7. Edmund Fontaine, *Governor's Message and Annual Reports of the Public Officers of the State* (Richmond, VA: Samuel Shepherd, 1848), 427–28.
8. As of publication, 249 enslaved people have been documented. The figure excludes uncountable groups of people known to labor for Blue Ridge Railroad contractors.
9. Wm. M. Sclater was William Morton Sclater, native of Fluvanna County, Virginia; Claudius Crozet to BPW, December 6, 1853, BRP.

10. Thanks to Jane C. Smith for her comparison of the unnoticed railroad at the University of Virginia with the forgotten laborers who built it.

Chapter 1

11. Receipts to John S. Cocke, April–December 1849, and G.A. Farrow, September–December 1849, BRP.
12. Claudius Crozet to President and Directors of the Blue Ridge Railroad Company, April 1, 1850, BRP.
13. Ibid., February 4, 1850; Jeremiah Wayland to Crozet, receipt for board of four men and a servant, June 1849, BRP.
14. Mary E. Lyons, *Claudius Crozet and the Blue Ridge Railroad: Selected Letters* (self-pub., 2017), Apple Book Store.
15. Ibid.; Crozet to James Brown, December 1, 1849, BRP.
16. Claudius Crozet, "Synopsis of Bids for the Eastern Division of the Blue Ridge Railroad," 1849, BRP.
17. Land compensation records, BRP; Federal Census, 1850, King William County, VA; James Whitney to C.P. Sanford, Richmond, VA, 1836, BRP.
18. Federal Census, 1850, Albemarle County, VA.
19. Kelly and Company contract with the Blue Ridge Railroad, December 1, 1849, BRP; John J. Zaborney, *Slaves for Hire: Renting Enslaved Laborers in Antebellum Virginia* (Baton Rouge: Louisiana State University Press, 2012), 126.
20. Claudius Crozet to BPW, May 11, 1849 and December 1, 1849, BRP; Crozet, Annual Report, October 1850, BRP.
21. Claudius Crozet to BPW, October 1850, BRP.
22. Claudius Crozet to James Brown, July 20, 1849, BRP; Crozet to BPW, October 1850, BRP; Section five on the Blue Ridge Railroad was followed by section six, which included Kelly's Cut and the Greenwood Tunnel. Blue Ridge Railroad payrolls indicate that no enslaved laborers toiled on sections five and six, other than making bricks for the Greenwood Tunnel.
23. Claudius Crozet to BPW, April 5, 1851, BRP.
24. Ibid., January 15, 1851.
25. Claudius Crozet, "Specifications for the Blue Ridge Railroad," specification 48, 1849, BRP.
26. Gregg D. Kimball, "African-Virginians and the Vernacular Building Tradition in Richmond City, 1790–1860," in *Perspectives in Vernacular Architecture, IV*, eds. Thomas Carter and Bernard L. Herman (Columbia: University of Missouri Press, 1991), 123.
27. Heidi Hackford, "Thomas Jefferson Randolph," https://www.monticello.org.
28. Ellen Wayles Randolph to Martha Jefferson Trist, April 17, 1849, Randolph Family Papers (hereafter cited as RFP), Accession no. 6225, Small Special Collections Library, University of Virginia. Thanks to Lucia Stanton, former senior historian at Monticello, for steering me toward Randolph papers related to the railroad.

29. Thomas Jefferson Randolph to editors of multiple Virginia newspapers, 1849, RFP; Christopher Valentine to Thomas Jefferson Randolph, December 20, 1849, RFP.
30. Claudius Crozet to President and Directors of the Blue Ridge Railroad Company, May 6, 1850, BRP; Crozet to BPW, January 15, 1851, BRP.
31. Federal Census Slave Schedule, Albemarle County, VA, 1850. Valentine posted his letters to Randolph from Yancey Mills, two miles south of sections seven and eight.
32. Claudius Crozet, "Specifications," specification 39, BRP.

Chapter 2

33. Ibid.; Claudius Crozet to President and Directors of the Blue Ridge Railroad, April 5, 1851, BRP; Crozet to BPW, July 16, 1851, BRP; Christopher Valentine to Thomas Jefferson Randolph, May 1, 1851, RFP.
34. Christopher Valentine to Thomas Jefferson Randolph, September 17, 1851, RFP; Claudius Crozet to Engineer's Office of the Blue Ridge Railroad, July 16, 1851, BRP.
35. Thomas Jefferson Randolph to BPW, May 2, 1854, BRP; William S. Carter to Christopher Valentine, July 13, 1854, BRP.
36. William S. Carter to Christopher Valentine, July 24, 1854, BRP; Thomas Jefferson Randolph to BPW, May 2, 1854, BRP.
37. Thomas Jefferson Randolph to BPW, May 2, 1854, BRP.
38. Edmund Myers to BPW, August 7, 1854, BRP; "A Synopsis of Bids for the Eastern Division of the Blue Ridge Railroad," 1849, BRP.
39. "Virginia Marriages 1851–1929," familysearch.org; Claudius Crozet to BPW, quarterly report, April 5, 1851, BRP.
40. Samuel McElroy was a merchant who boarded with Hugh Gallaher and other James River Canal personnel in Rockbridge County, 1850.
41. Wilma A. Dunaway, *Slavery in the American Mountain South* (Cambridge, UK: Cambridge University Press, 2003), 90–91; R.L. Walker and Hugh L. Gallaher to BPW, December 12, 1851, BRP. Reuben Lindsay Walker (1827–1890) was born in Albemarle County, Virginia, and graduated from Virginia Military Institute in 1845.
42. "Questions Propounded to H.L. Gallaher by C. Crozet, and the answers of Mr. Gallaher," January 18, 1851, BRP; Claudius Crozet to BPW, October 3, 1853, BRP; Little Rock Tunnel and Robinson's [Robertson] Hollow account book, 1854, BRP. In addition to drills, laborers on section four used crowbars, hammers, fuse and blasting powder.
43. "Blue Ridge Railroad Company Section 2 contract Mordecai Sizer," transfer to George Farrow, September 25, 1852, and Robert P. Smith, February 10, 1853, BRP; Federal Census, 1850, Albemarle County, VA.
44. Mary E. Lyons, *The Virginia Blue Ridge Railroad* (Charleston, SC: The History Press, 2015), 61; Federal Census Agricultural Schedule, Albemarle County, VA, 1850.

Chapter 3

45. Charles Ellet, *The Mountain Top Track: A Description of the Railroad Across the Blue Ridge at Rockfish Gap in the State of Virginia* (Philadelphia: T.K and P.G. Collins, 1856), 8–10.

46. Ibid.

47. Ibid.; Lyons, *Virginia Blue Ridge Railroad*, 70–71, 79; Claudius Crozet to William. R. Drinkard, Secretary of BPW, April 22, 1853, BRP.

48. Claudius Crozet to BPW, December 6, 1853, BRP.

49. Louis Spilman, "If the First Hundred Years Are the Hardest, Uncle Jim Should Know," *Waynesboro News Virginian*, December 7, 1939, 7.

50. Federal Census Slave Schedule, Albemarle County, VA, 1850; Spilman, "First Hundred Years."

51. Spilman, "First Hundred Years."

52. Ibid.; Claudius Crozet, "Remarks Relative to Mr. R.P. Smith's Bill," May 7, 1855, BRP.

53. Claudius Crozet, "Specifications," specification 87, BRP.

54. Spilman, "First Hundred Years."

55. Claudius Crozet to BPW, September 5, November 8, December 6, 1853, BRP.

56. Blue Ridge Railroad payroll, 31 east, September 1853, BRP.

57. Claudius Crozet to BPW, August 2, 1853, BRP; Claiborne Rice Mason (1801–1885) was tracklayer for the Virginia Central Railroad temporary track. He likely used slave labor again for the eponymous Mason Tunnel, located farther west on the Virginia Central line in Bath County.

58. Claudius Crozet to Charles Ellet, January 18, 1854, BRP. "Mr. Smith" was William Smith, brother of Robert P. Smith.

59. McElroy estimate, March 1853, BRP; R.L. Walker estimate, August 1853, BRP.

60. Claudius Crozet to BPW, July 6, 1852, BRP.

61. Claudius Crozet to the President and Directors of the Blue Ridge Railroad, November 30, 1849, BRP; Mary E. Lyons, "Cemetery by the Tracks: An Unsolved Mystery," *Crozet Gazette*, July 6, 2016.

62. "Contract for the Grading, Masonry, Etc. of the Blue Ridge Railroad from the End of the 8th Section to the Foot of the Blue Ridge. Articles of Agreement," September 30, 1851, 3, BRP; Claudius Crozet to BPW, December 6, 1853, BRP.

63. Claudius Crozet to BPW, July 6, 1852, BRP.

64. "Blue Ridge Railroad Contract for Ballasting and Trimming from Mechum's River to the Third Tunnel," March 18, 1853, BRP; W.P. Bocock, opinion regarding William S. Carter, December 14, 1853, BRP.

65. "Articles of Agreement between Robert P. Smith and the Blue Ridge Railroad," March 18, 1853, BRP; Claudius Crozet to BPW, May 7, 1855, BRP; Crozet to BPW, December 6, 1853, BRP.

66. Federal Census, Albemarle County, VA, 1850; Federal Census Slave Schedule, Albemarle County, VA, 1850; Wallace general store ledger, Greenwood, VA, 1852, private collection; Blue Ridge Railroad ledger, September 1852, 23, BRP.

67. Claudius Crozet to BPW, August 2 and December 6, 1853, BRP.

68. Ibid., November 8, 1853.
69. Ibid., December 6, 1853.
70. Lyons, *Virginia Blue Ridge Railroad*, 11–13; Claudius Crozet to BPW, January 4, 1854, BRP.
71. BPW Journal, November 1853, BRP.
72. *Richmond Daily Dispatch*, August 4, 1852, virginiachronicle.com; *Richmond Daily Dispatch*, December 28, 1854, virginiachronicle.com; Claudius Crozet to BPW, January 4, 1854, BRP.
73. Claudius Crozet to BPW, January 4, 1854, BRP. The spelling of Hansbrough's surname is based on his signature.
74. Ibid.

Chapter 4

75. Claudius Crozet to William R. Drinkard, April 22, 1853, BRP; Crozet to BPW, June 3, 1854, BRP.
76. Claudius Crozet to BPW, March 11, 1853, BRP; Scott Reynolds Nelson, *Steel Drivin' Man: John Henry, the Untold Story of an American Legend* (New York: Oxford University Press, 2006), 83; Coffey, "Into the Valley," 15.
77. Coffey, "Into the Valley," 14.
78. Blue Ridge Railroad payrolls, 1854, BRP; Claudius Crozet to BPW, February 8, 1854, BRP.
79. Blue Ridge Railroad payrolls, 1854, BRP; Willis M. Carter, *Journal*, ca. 1894, Willis M. Carter digital collection, Library of Virginia, 11.
80. Coffey, "Into the Valley," 15; Blue Ridge Railroad payrolls, 1854, BRP.
81. Plat map, Isaac Womaldorf estate, Nelson County Courthouse, Lovingston, VA, deed book 17, 170; Carter, *Journal*, 4, 8.
82. Contract between John Kelly and Blue Ridge Railroad, December 1, 1849, BRP.
83. James Jarman, affidavit, Richmond, VA, March 6, 1855, BRP.
84. "Socrates Maupin," University of Virginia Library, https://explore.lib.virginia.edu.; Zaborney, *Slaves for Hire*, 73; Federal Census, Henrico County, VA, 1850; contract between Claudius Crozet and Socrates Maupin, January 1, 1854, BRP.
85. Federal Census, Albemarle County, VA, 1850; "Agreed Rate of Medical Charges," *Physician Price Fixing in 19th Century Virginia* (blog), http://blog.hsl.virginia.ed.; "John Singleton Mosby," American Battlefield Trust, https://www.civilwar.org.; contract between Claudius Crozet and A.D. Mosby, July 17, 1854, BRP.
86. "Chs. Carter," *Physician Price Fixing in 19th Century Virginia* (blog), http://blog.hsl.virginia.edu; Federal Census Slave Schedule, Albemarle County, VA, 1850; "Old Colored Citizen Dead," *Charlottesville Daily Progress*, December 7, 1899; contract between Claudius Crozet and Charles Carter, January 1, 1854, BRP.
87. Federal Census Slave Schedule, Albemarle County, VA, 1850; https://www.monticello.org/site/jefferson/thomas-jefferson-randolph; Thomas Jefferson Randolph to BPW, July 14, 1854, BRP.

88. Thomas Jefferson Randolph to BPW, May 2, 1854 and July 14, 1854, BRP.

89. Thomas Jefferson Randolph, "Speech of Thomas J. Randolph in the House of Delegates of Virginia: On the Abolition of Slavery" (speech), 1832 https://www.loc.gov.

90. Thomas Jefferson Randolph to BPW, May 2, 1854, BRP.

91. James Alexander, *Charlottesville Jeffersonian Republican*, March 22, 1854; *Lexington Gazette*, March 30, 1854.

92. Claudius Crozet to BPW, April 29, 1854, BRP; W.P. Bocock, attorney general, opinion for the Board of Public Works, November 1, 1854, BRP. Willis Perry Bocock (1797–1866) was attorney general for Virginia from 1852 to 1857.

93. Bocock, opinion for the BPW.

94. Claudius Crozet to BPW, April 29, 1854, BRP.

95. Bocock, opinion for BPW.

96. Ibid.

97. Ibid.

98. Testimony regarding the deaths of Jerry and Tom, November 1, 1854, BRP.

99. Ibid.

100. Ibid.

101. Claudius Crozet to BPW, April 29, 1854, BRP.

102. Testimony regarding the deaths of Jerry and Tom, November 1, 1854, BRP.

103. William Sclater to John Maupin, May 26, 1854, BRP.

104. Claudius Crozet to BPW, June 3, 1854, BRP.

105. B.W. Starke, Notary Public, affidavits of George D. Harris, William Sclater, and James H. Jarman, Richmond, VA, March 6, 1855, BRP.

106. Ibid.

107. Ibid.

108. Ibid.

109. August and Randolph [Attorneys], to BPW, March 31, 1855, BRP.

110. Ibid.

111. Ibid.

112. For more about possible cemeteries for enslaved Blue Ridge Railroad laborers, see Mary E. Lyons, *The Blue Ridge Tunnel: A Remarkable Engineering Feat in Antebellum Virginia* (Charleston, SC: The History Press, 2014), 89–102; Lyons, "Cemetery by the Tracks."

113. Lyons, *Blue Ridge Tunnel*, 107; Blue Ridge Railroad payroll, east side, July 1854, BRP.

114. Blue Ridge Railroad east side payrolls, July–August 1854, BRP; *Richmond Enquirer*, August 15, 1854.

115. Blue Ridge Railroad east side payrolls, September–December 1854, BRP.

116. Claudius Crozet to BPW, December 1, 1854, BRP.

117. Ibid.

118. Ibid.

119. Claudius Crozet to BPW, December 28, 1854, BRP.

120. Ibid.

121. Ibid.

Chapter 5

122. *Richmond Enquirer*, "Accident in the Tunnel," February 6, 1855, http:///www.virginiamemory.com; Claudius Crozet to BPW, March 31, 1855, BRP.

123. Claudius Crozet to BPW, March 31, 1855, BRP.

124. Blue Ridge Railroad payrolls, January and February 1855, BRP.

125. Coffey, "Into the Valley," 15.

126. Blue Ridge Railroad east side payrolls, January 1855, July 1855, BRP.

127. Blue Ridge Railroad east side payrolls, 1855, 1856, BRP; Zaborney, *Slaves for Hire*, 65–66.

128. Spilman, "First Hundred Years."

129. James Alexander, *Early Charlottesville Recollections of James Alexander 1828–1874* (Charlottesville, VA: Albemarle County Historical Society, 1942). First published *Jeffersonian Republican* 1942 by Michie Company (Charlottesville, VA), 102.

130. *Richmond Daily Dispatch* 8, no. 18, July 23, 1855, http:///www.virginiamemory.com; D.D.T. Leech, comp., *Post Office Directory, or Businessman's Guide to Post Offices in the United States* (New York: J.H. Colton and Company, 1856), 179; "Asleep on the Track," *Richmond Daily Dispatch*, May 19, 1854, http:///www.virginiamemory.com.

131. Spilman, "First Hundred Years"; Douglas Wilson, Lincoln Studies Center, Knox College, Galesburg, IL, to Paul Collinge, November 5, 2018.

132. Spilman, "First Hundred Years."

133. Ellet, *Mountain Top Track*, 22; Claudius Crozet to BPW, November 14, 1856, BRP.

134. Claudius Crozet to BPW, November 14, 1856, BRP.

135. Federal Census Agricultural Schedule, Augusta County, VA, 1850.

136. "Wills, 1865 Sampson Pelter of Augusta Co VA USA," Chancery Records Index 1877–029, http://www.virginiamemory.com; Pelter collection of J.B. Yount III, Library of Virginia.

137. Chancery Records Index Numbers 1845–009 and 1857–057, Library of Virginia; photograph of Sampson Pelter house, estate of Joseph Bryon Yount, Waynesboro, VA, DeYoung Auctions.

138. Claudius Crozet to James Brown Jr., BPW, March 18, 1850, BRP.

139. Samuel B. Brown to Claudius Crozet, February 28, 1850, BRP.

140. Ibid.; "Wills, 1865 Sampson Pelter," http://www.virginiamemory.com.

141. Claudius Crozet to BPW, April 5, 1851, BRP; Blue Ridge Railroad payrolls, BRP; Blue Ridge Railroad account book, BRP.

142. Kelly and Company, contractors' estimate for Blue Ridge Tunnel, December 1856, BRP. Under the remarks column, a handwritten notation states, "Progress. Heading perforated on the 29th Decr. 1856."

Chapter 6

143. Claudius Crozet to President and Directors of the Blue Ridge Railroad, November 30, 1849, BRP.

144. Crozet, "Specifications," specification 40, 1849, BRP.

145. James Poyntz Nelson, *Claudius Crozet: His Story of the Four Tunnels in the Blue Ridge Region of Virginia on the Chesapeake and Ohio Railway Constructed 1849–1858* (Richmond, VA: Mitchell and Hotchkiss, 1917), 5; Claudius Crozet to BPW, September 1, 1854, BRP; E.C. Howard to Crozet, June 30, 1852, BRP; Rick Bonomo, Brick Collecting, https://brickcollecting.com.

146. Bonomo, Brick Collecting.

147. Ibid.

148. E.C. Howard to Crozet, June 30, 1852, BRP.

149. Ibid.; Crozet, memorandum, July 7, 1852, BRP; Crozet to BPW, September 1, 1854, BRP; Federal Census Slave Schedules, Albemarle and Louisa Counties, VA, 1850; Federal Census, Louisa County, 1850.

150. Claudius Crozet to BPW, January 26, 1854; October 2, 1854; January 1, 1858, BRP.

151. Federal Census, Fluvanna County, VA, 1850, 1860; Federal Census Slave Schedules, Fluvanna County VA, 1850, 1860; Claudius Crozet to BPW, December 9, 1855, BRP.

152. Claudius Crozet to BPW, April 21, 1857, BRP.

153. Ibid.

154. Ibid.

155. Ibid., May 20, 1857.

156. Ibid., April 21, 1857, May 20, 1857; Federal Census and Slave Schedule, Louisa County, VA, 1850.

157. Federal Census, Louisa County, VA, 1860; Claudius Crozet to BPW, May 20, 1857, BRP.

158. Citizens of Augusta County, VA, to BPW, June 1857, July 23, 1857, BRP; J. Garret, Secretary of Board of Directors of Virginia Central Railroad Company, board minutes, July 21, 1857, BRP.

159. Claudius Crozet to BPW, January 1, 1858, BRP; William Couper, *Southern Sketches Number 8, First Series, Claudius Crozet Soldier-Scholar-Educator-Engineer (1789–1864)* (Charlottesville, VA: Historical Publishing Co., 1936), 174–75.

160. *Doc. No. XVII. Fourth Biennial and Forty-First Report of the Board of Public Works to the General Assembly of Virginia with the Accompanying Documents*, 1859, 13.

161. At an undetermined time after arching under Claudius Crozet's authority was completed, an additional 694 feet were arched in the Blue Ridge Tunnel. See Rogers, "Preliminary Stability Assessment," 123.

Chapter 7

162. Federal Census, Albemarle County, VA, 1850, 1860.

163. Rogers, "Preliminary Stability Assessment," 52.

164. Spilman, "First Hundred Years."

165. Ibid.

166. Federal Census Slave Schedule, Albemarle County, VA, 1860; Spilman, "First Hundred Years"; Carter, *Journal*, 11.

167. Spilman, "First Hundred Years."

168. For adolescent escapes, see Wallace Turnage, *A Slave No More: Two Men Who Escaped to Freedom Including Their Own Narratives of Emancipation*, David W. Blight, ed. (New York: Harcourt Brace and Co., 2007); Harriet Jacobs, *Incidents in the Life of a Slave Girl*, Jean Yellin, ed. (Boston: Harvard University Press, 1987); Zaborney, *Slaves for Hire*, 6, 78.

169. Spilman, "First Hundred Years."

170. Ibid.

171. Ibid.

172. Edmund Fontaine, Annual Report of the Virginia Central Railroad, 1850, quoted by Charles W. Turner, *Chessie's Road* (Richmond, VA: Garret and Massie, 1956), 39.

173. Turner, *Chessie's Road*, 43; Edmund Fontaine, *Annual Report to the Stockholders*, 1862, quoted by Turner, *Chessie's Road*, 58.

174. Ibid., 45.

175. Spilman, "The First Hundred Years."

176. Ibid.

177. Ibid.

Chapter 8

178. Federal Census, Albemarle County VA, 1870, 1880.

179. "Sanborn Insurance Map from Charlottesville, Independent Cities, Virginia, New York," Sanborn Map Company, July 1891, http://hdl.loc.gov; Federal Census, Albemarle County, VA, 1870, 1880.

180. *Acts and Joint Resolutions Passed by the State of Virginia During the Session of 1885–'86* (Richmond, VA: A.R. Micou, Superintendent of Public Printing, 1886), 15; Barefoot, *Corner*, 72; J.H Beadle, *Western Wilds, and the Men Who Redeem Them* (Cincinnati, OH: Jones Brothers and Co., 1880), 53. "I took a position as engineer of a six-mule team."

181. "Old Colored Citizen Dead," *Charlottesville Daily Progress*, December 7, 1899; "Railroads," Charlottesville: A Brief History, http://www2.iath.virginia.edu; Federal Census, Albemarle County, VA, 1870, 1880; J.F. Bell Funeral Home Records, http://www2.vcdh. Thanks to Jane C. Smith for locating the obituary for Remus Bracket.

182. George A. Farrow family daybook, private collection; Lyons, "Brooksville African-American Community, 1820–1880," unpublished compilation, 2013. The six family groups were Hailstock, Cross, Rodes, Spears, Stewart and White.

183. Federal Census, Albemarle County, VA, 1870, 1880; Freedmen's Bureau, familysearch.org, data extracted by Sam Towler.

184. Carter, *Journal*, 11–12.

185. Ibid., 14–22.

186. Ibid.

187. Ibid.; "Wills, 1865 Sampson Pelter," http://www.virginiamemory.com.

188. Chancery Records Index 015-1890-034, http://www.virginiamemory.com.

189. Spilman, "First Hundred Years."

190. Ibid.; Federal Census, Augusta County, VA, 1880, 1900.

191. Deed book 122, 209, Augusta County Court House, Staunton, VA; Federal Census, Augusta County, VA, 1900; Spilman, "First Hundred Years"; Ethel Kay Sandridge, untitled (unpublished manuscript, August 27, 1941), 2; The dirt road to Crimora is now the Eastside Highway.

192. Israel Gillette Jefferson and S.F. Wetmore, "Life Among the Lowly, No. 3," *Pike County Republican*, December 25, 1873.

193. Thomas Jefferson Randolph to *Pike County Republican*, https://www.encyclopediavirginia.org.

194. Ibid.

195. Kathleen Golden, "Meet John S. Mosby, 'Gray Ghost' of the Confederacy," *O Say Can You See?* (blog), National Museum of American History, http://americanhistory.si.edu; "Chs. Carter," *Physician Price Fixing in 19th Century Virginia*; "Socrates Maupin," University of Virginia Library; Wolfe, "Slavery at the University of Virginia"; Ann Freudenberg and John Casteen, eds., "John B. Minor's Civil War Diary," *Magazine of Albemarle County History Civil War Issue* 22 (1964): 49.

196. Gene D. Lewis, *Charles Ellet, Jr.: The Engineer as Individualist 1810–1862* (Urbana: University of Illinois Press, 1968), 73, 200, 207.

197. Robert F. Hunter and Edward L. Dooley, *Claudius Crozet: French Engineer in America, 1790–1864* (Charlottesville: University Press of Virginia, 1989), 178; Sean Patrick Adams, "Claudius Crozet," *Dictionary of Virginia Biography*, Vol. 3, Sara B. Bears, ed. (Richmond: Library of Virginia, 2006), 582.

198. Federal Census, Albemarle County, VA, 1860; Jarman descendant to the author, October 29, 2018; Federal Census, Nelson County, VA, 1870.

199. Sam Towler, "New York: Albemarle," unpublished typescript, 2014, 27; George A. Farrow family daybook, private collection; Confederate Applications for Presidential Pardons 1865–1867 for George A. Farrow; U.S. Pardons Under Amnesty Proclamations 1865–1869 for George A. Farrow; Death Indexing Project, Virginia Genealogical Society, Library of Virginia; U.S. Southern Claims Commission Master Index 1871–1880 for George A. Farrow.

Chapter 9

200. Spilman, "First Hundred Years."

201. Ibid.

202. Ibid.

203. Ibid.

204. Kaytlin Nickens, "Virginia Expresses a 'Profound Regret' for Lynchings," *Charlottesville Daily Progress*, February 12, 2019; Sterling Giles and Brian Williams, "Map of Virginia's Lynching History," *Virginia Commonwealth University Capital*

News Service, 2019. The deceased included John Henry James, lynched in Albemarle County next to former Virginia Central Railroad tracks in 1898; "John Henry James," Jefferson School, American Heritage Center, https://jeffschoolheritagecenter.org.

205. Hermond Norwood, "Fountain Hughes" in *Voices from the Days of Slavery: Stories Songs and Memories*, produced by Guha Shankar, American Folklife Center and Lisa Carl, transcript, https://www.loc.gov.

206. Spilman, "First Hundred Years."

207. Ibid.

208. Joe Nutt, *Historical Sketches of African-American Churches (Past and Present) of Augusta County, Staunton, Waynesboro, & Vicinity: Including Cemetery Burial Records and Biographies* (Staunton, VA: Community Involvement Awareness, 2001), 235–36; Jed Hotchkiss, "Map of Middle River Magisterial District," in *Historical Atlas, Augusta County, Virginia* (Chicago: Waterman, Watkins and Co., 1886), 77.

209. Nutt, *Historical Sketches*. For a full account of destruction of the Wesley/Belvidere Cemetery, see Lynn Rainville, *Hidden History: African American Cemeteries in Central Virginia* (Charlottesville: University of Virginia Press, 2014), 11–15.

210. Rainville, *Hidden History*, 11, 49.

Epilogue

211. Norfolk Branch, Virginia Section, American Society of Civil Engineers to Committee on the History and Heritage of American Civil Engineering, December 25, 1971; C.M. Sawyer to L. Neal Fitzsimons, "The Crozet Tunnel: A Proposal for Landmark Status, Supplement 1–2, January 1976."

212. C.M. Sawyer to L. Neal Fitzsimons, February 12, 1976; Robert M. Vogel to Carl E. Betterton, September 7, 1971.

213. American Society of Civil Engineers Public Information Services press release, May 21, 1976, 4.

214. C.M. Sawyer to L. Neal Fitzsimons.

Appendix 1

215. Irishman John Kelly and his countryman John Larguey were contractors for the Blue Ridge, Brooksville and Greenwood Tunnels on the Blue Ridge Railroad.

216. L.S., abbreviation for Latin *locus sigilli*, meaning "place of the seal."

Appendix 2

217. *Waynesboro News Virginian*, Friday, January 22, 1943.

218. "Ex-slave Is Found Dead," *Waynesboro News Virginian*, February 20, 1943.

219. Samuel F. Diggs, "News of Our Colored Folks," *Waynesboro News Virginian*.

INDEX

Index

ABOUT THE AUTHOR

Mary E. Lyons has written nineteen award-winning books for young readers about slavery, the Irish famine and the ancient American world. Most recently, she is the author of *The Blue Ridge Tunnel: A Remarkable Engineering Feat in Antebellum Virginia* and *The Virginia Blue Ridge Railroad*, both published by The History Press. She lives in Charlottesville, Virginia, with her husband, Paul.